Spiritual Classics

Spiritual Classics

Magpie Books, London

Constable & Robinson Ltd
3 The Lanchesters
162 Fulham Palace Road
London W6 9ER

This edition published by Magpie Books,
an imprint of Constable & Robinson Ltd 2009

A copy of the British Library Cataloguing in Publication Data
is available from the British Library

ISBN 978-1-84529-785-5

Printed and bound in the European Union

1 3 5 7 9 10 8 6 4 2

Mixed Sources
Product group from well-managed
forests and other controlled sources
www.fsc.org Cert no. SA-COC-1565
© 1996 Forest Stewardship Council
FSC

Contents

Introduction

The aim of this book is to provide brief introductions to some of the world's spiritual classics. This immediately raises two questions: "What is a spiritual classic?" and "How widely should we cast our net in choosing the selection of books to be covered?"

We have taken the view that there is no simple answer to the question of what constitutes a spiritual classic. There are many obvious candidates among the religious literature of the world. We have chosen not to include any religious scripture, in other words there are no selections from the Bible, or from the sacred books of any other religion. Instead these are books that are in one sense or another concerned with spirituality, theology, or matters of faith.

By necessity the choice is an eclectic one. Every editor would make a different selection when presented with this task, and no one can claim that their choice is definitive. A brief list of those whose books haven't been included makes it clear how difficult the choice was. We haven't included Martin Luther or Ignatius of Loyola, nor George MacDonald or Thomas a Kempis. There was no room for John Wesley, Sheldon Vanauken, Pheobe Palmer, or Sundar Singh. Every one of these writers (and a hundred more besides) have written books that can rightly be regarded as classics. Meanwhile some books have been included here because they are or have been regarded as classics of their sort, even though the present editor would regard them as of less value than the writers mentioned above.

Rather than attempt the impossible we have chosen to celebrate the wide range of spiritual writing that can be read for enjoyment or inspiration, including some books that come from beyond religious tradition, including novels, and more than one title that can be regarded as a book for children. We have tried to focus on important works while recognizing that people find spiritual enlightenment and succor in a wide variety of books.

This leads us on to the second question confronted in making the selections for this book. We are writing from within the Christian tradition, but should one go out of one's way to try to present a neutral view of "spirituality around the world"? And how should we deal with the many different strands and beliefs that exist within Christianity itself?

It is far beyond the scope of this book to present a history of the Christian church. Nonetheless we have to acknowledge that there have been many different beliefs grouped under the umbrella of Christianity. We have included books from many different parts of the Christian church over the centuries, including medieval mysticism, Quakers, modern evangelists, Protestant and Catholic alike. We have intentionally avoided giving any particular kind of Christian belief priority over others. This is not intended as a clumsy attempt at ecumenical inclusiveness, merely to reflect the fact that inspired and fascinating thinkers have emerged from all different facets of Christian history.

Moving beyond Christianity, the last two sections of the book explore secular spirituality and writings from different religious traditions. Rather than make any attempt to include a representation of every type of world religion or belief, we have chosen an interesting range of titles that seem to have some specific interest or message that reaches beyond their religious origins.

These are intended as examples of titles that may be of interest to anyone who has a broad interest in matters of spirituality and religion. Of course, as with the Christian texts, it is impossible to claim any kind of completeness or to deny that many other books could equally have been included. We can only hope that the opportunity arises to write a second volume of this book in which all those books that we didn't find room for this time can be included.

Each book that we have chosen is described in a few pages. It can be hard to capture the essence of a book in such a short space. Our guiding principle was to try to explain the books in such a way as to convey a brief idea of what each one has to offer the interested reader. But also we wanted to answer the question "Would I enjoy and understand this book?" which sometimes involves trying to explain the strengths and weaknesses of the book for a modern reader.

The 'Speed Reads' included at the end of each entry aim to deliver a quick sense of what the writer is like to read. They also provide a highly compressed summary of the main points of the book in question.

Overall we have aimed for a chatty and comprehensible style, even if this occasionally risks criticism for being insufficiently serious. We have tried to explain the books as we would to an interested friend, rather than taking too academic a viewpoint, and we hope that this makes for a readable and interesting journey.

Each book section is self-contained, and there is no reason why the book shouldn't be used as a reference of for dipping into. However we have also arranged the book into seven sections, grouping the books together in various ways. Within each section the books are arranged chronologically. While there is no attempt at a joined-up historical approach, the chronological progression at times shows up some interesting juxtapositions, and relations between the books included.

There are a couple of general editorial points to be made. Firstly many of these books are available in a variety of editions and with alternative titles. Where this is an issue we have aimed to use the most commonly used title. Publication dates are also sometimes uncertain – we have used first publication where this is known, but obviously for some of the earlier books the best we can do is give the correct century or decade. In a few cases the quote given at the start of the section is not from the specific book under discussion – this is in cases where the best way to give a flavour of the author's writing seemed to be to use an alternative quote from their other writings.

In conclusion, we hope that the final book is one that will provide entertainment and inspiration and one that will be a useful, if idiosyncratic guide to a representative selection of the many wonderful spiritual books that have been written over the centuries.

Early Christian Classics

Early Christian Classics: Introduction

THE HISTORY OF THE early Christian church is an endlessly fascinating story. From the early days of persecution in the Roman Empire, through legalisation in the fourth century, and the gradual spread of the gospel through subsequent centuries, Christianity survived and prospered through some dark times in history. The attitudes of the very early Christians are represented here by two fascinating texts, *The Sayings of the Desert Fathers* and *The City of God*. Both cast a great deal of light on the early history of the church.

In the latter part of the first millennium, following the collapse of the Roman Empire, the church became a major political player in Europe, while the monastic movement developed the theology and philosophy that underpinned the religion.

This was the period in which the Christian church established its dominion over much of Europe, went into battle with the more recent Islamic church in the crusades, established the Inquisition to suppress the unorthodox, and ultimately separated in the

Eastern and Roman branches of the church in a schism that remains in place today.

In this period, Christianity was primarily a paternalistic religion in which the message of Christ was interpreted for ordinary people by the priesthood. Within the Roman church, masses and bibles continued to be propagated in the Latin, even as the language died as an everyday tongue and became a historical relic. There are of course many fascinating texts from this period, although the scholastic theology can be dense and hard to empathize with today.

From a modern perspective, it is more interesting to look at some of the books that started to emerge from about the fourteenth century onwards. From a distance the books of orthodoxy are less interesting than those thinkers who tried to understand their own personal relationship with God. Writers such as Meister Eckhart and Marguerite Porete departed from the orthodox teaching of the church to one degree or another and suffered the consequences. From this time onwards the invention of the printing press also meant that unorthodox ideas were able to circulate in a way that had been difficult in the middle ages.

It is perhaps not surprising that the most enduring writing of this period was produced by thinkers who were starting to question the established church in one way or another. Teresa of Avila and St John of the Cross were reacting against the luxury and decadence of their contemporaries in the church when they founded the Discalced Carmelites. Even John Bunyan, who was writing after the establishment of the Protestant Church of England, was fighting for his own puritan ideals against the orthodoxy of his own country.

In this section of the book we encounter some mysticism, several puritanical approaches, and the "back-to-basics" Christianity of St Francis, who dared to take Christ at his word when he implored his followers to spread the word without shoes or money. Several of the authors in this section were condemned as heretical in their time and others such as Teresa of Avila and St Francis had to battle for their views against stubborn opposition.

To the modern reader the appeal of these books is to see the individual struggling with the demands of trying to live a good life, attempting to reach their own understanding of Christ's message and their own comprehension of the divine, rather than simply relying on received wisdom. Rather than regarding the individualism of these writers as heresy or unorthodoxy, we can understand that they are aiming to reach a more complete and authentic understanding of their spirituality.

There is also a great deal of poetry and beauty in titles such as *The Little Flowers of St. Francis* and *Dark Night of the Soul,* while *The Pilgrim's Progress* has been a hugely influential work of fiction over the subsequent centuries. Beyond their spiritual message, these books are a reminder of the huge contribution that spiritual writing has made to the cultural and intellectual development of the modern world.

Sayings of the Desert Fathers,
Fourth Century
The Desert Fathers

"Let us charge into the good fight with joy and love without being afraid of our enemies. Though unseen themselves, they can look at the face of our soul, and if they see it altered by fear, they take up arms against us all the more fiercely. For the cunning creatures have observed that we are scared. So let us take up arms against them courageously. No one will fight with a resolute fighter."

FOR AN INSIGHT into the attitudes of the very early church, there is no better place to start than with the sayings of the Desert Fathers, which have been published in a variety of collections, sometimes under the Latin name of *Apophthegmata Patrum*. The Desert Fathers were those hermits, monks, and ascetics who lived a few centuries after Christ, and chose to follow monastic or eremitic lives in the desert region of Egypt, from the third century onwards. At this stage the life and work of Christ was relatively recent history, so it is fascinating to see the beliefs and practices of the Desert Fathers.

They had mostly fled from the persecution of the Roman Empire, which was going through a turbulent period, for which reason Christians were frequently scapegoated. The reign of the emperor Diocletian was a particularly brutal one for early followers of Christ and as a result the religion became a fugitive one, operating in small refugee communities away from the urban centers.

Christianity became legal in the Roman Empire in 313 AD, under Emperor Constantine, but while many people were now free to live openly as Christians, some continued the solitary lives that they had developed during the harsher years. The desert had a great appeal as a place where people could live in stoic simplicity – the story of Christ's temptation and fasting on the mountain with John the Baptist was one that resonated deeply with the early Christians. To a degree they were attempting to recreate the deprivations of his time there. They were also continuing religious traditions of asceticism that were already in existence and adapting these to a specifically Christian way of life.

By living in isolation in the desert and exercizing extreme self-discipline, they hoped to follow in the path of Jesus, rejecting worldly pleasures and seeking a closer relationship with God. The Desert Fathers were revered for their wisdom and holiness, and this was the reason for their sayings and deeds being collected by early writers. They are also fascinating because their practices were so individual and idiosyncratic. For instance, Simeon Stylites chose to live for 37 years on a platform perched on top of a pole, to find a pure form of solitude and sacrifice. This seems almost comical now, but it is an example of the extremes of devout behavior that were evident in the Desert Fathers.

Over time, their lives as hermits became more formal and less solitary and, under the influence of significant figures such as Anthony the Great and Pachomius, a life of common prayer and meals, together with solitary prayer and meditation was starting to form the basis of the Christian monastic tradition. The basic idea of the fathers – that we can ascend to God through a mixture of self-sacrifice, abstinence, and meditation leading to spiritual progress – became a fundamental model of Christian practice that is still influential today.

One modern figure who edited a collection of their sayings was Thomas Merton, who is known for a twentieth-century exposition of the virtues of the monastic life and solitude. As a young man he had aspired to live a life as holy as those of the Desert Fathers.

The various collections that can be bought give different

selections of the source material. Some of the collections divide the material by subject matters, others by the father (or mother) to whom sayings and deeds are ascribed.

One thing that the sayings of the Desert Fathers can't be seen as is reliable history. The collections were originally passed down from the Coptic church, via Greek translations, and it is impossible to know if the sayings and deeds ascribed to particular fathers are accurate. But from any of these collections one gets a general impression of the beliefs and acts of these individuals and the state of the church in their lifetimes.

The sayings cover a wide range of theological and spiritual areas. Obviously there is an emphasis on the ascetic life. There is also a tendency for some of the stories of deprivations and suffering welcomed by the fathers to seem somewhat grotesque and masochistic by modern standards. However, one can't help but be impressed by the hardiness of those who were prepared to undergo these deprivations in the name of their beliefs. There are also inevitable moments of misogyny, as the temptation of women is regarded with great horror by these fathers. But this has to be seen within the context of the period.

Another aspect of the sayings which is inspiring in a modern context is the extraordinary perseverance that these fathers show in their attitude to spiritual progress. St John of the Ladder writes:

> *Do not be surprised that you fall every day; do not give up, but stand your ground courageously. And assuredly, the angel who guards you will honour your patience.*

Today we can find great inspiration in such attitudes even if we are unlikely to follow the Desert Fathers to their extremes of asceticism. Jesus said "Deny yourself, take up your cross and follow me." Today we rarely take these words as seriously as the early church did, but in reading the lives of the Desert Fathers we can see the example of believers who took every word of Jesus' exhortation with full seriousness.

Another respect in which we can take inspiration from the

desert fathers today is with regard to temptation. Anyone who tries to live a good life may know the problem of temptation, whether this be from failing to live up to one's own expectations, from the temptations of sensuality, over-eating, laziness, or whatever may be our personal weaknesses.

Since the Desert Fathers tried to live such ascetic existences, they were constantly faced with the problem of temptation, as even an additional crumb of food might count for them as a failure within their personal goals. Abba Isaiah the Solitary wrote:

> *When you pray to God in time of temptation do not say, 'Take this . . . away from me', but pray like this: 'O Jesus Christ, sovereign Master, help me and do not let me sin against Thee . . .'*

Rather than imploring Jesus to deliver him from temptation, Abba Isaiah is suggesting that we should concentrate on the imperative not to sin, and thus overcome the temptation even when it remains with us. This is a powerful approach to the problem of how to deal with temptation – to pray for the temptation to be taken from us implies that we are not strong enough to reject it. Whereas to pray for Christ's help in avoiding sin suggests that our desire to avoid sin should be powerful enough to overcome the temptation no matter what, which is a far stronger faith.

The power of the sayings of the Desert Fathers today lies in many such small moments of contemplation. The sayings make an ideal accompaniment to prayer and meditation as they can be read in short bursts and each moment inspires us to consider different aspects of faith and belief. Some moments in the book may seem to be from an era that is long past, but other thoughts and ideas in the book remain as true to day as they were all those centuries ago.

Sayings of the Desert Fathers

The Speed Read

The collected sayings and deeds of the early Christian hermits, monks, and ascetics who lived in the Scetes desert in the fourth century AD, either in solitude or in small groups overseen by an elder. Undertaking lives of asceticism and holiness, they represent an extreme but powerful representation of early Christianity, and their sayings retain great power to inspire and teach us today.

City of God, Fifth Century
Augustine

*"Though there are very many nations all over the earth,
. . . there are no more than two kinds of human society,
which we may justly call two cities . . . one consisting of
those who live according to man, the other of those who
live according to God . . . To the City of Man belong the
enemies of God . . . so inflamed with hatred against the
City of God."*

ONE OF THE MOST interesting medieval thinkers was
Augustine of Hippo. A North African who converted to
Christianity, he has to be understood within the specific
intellectual culture of his time. Many writers' main concern was to
harmonize Christian ideas with the thinking of the Greek philosophers, Plato in particular.

The Egyptian writer Plotinus is often seen as the foremost inter-
preter of Plato in a Christian context in this period, but the task he
set himself was one that many attempted – to provide a rational
foundation for the mystical and theological aspects of Christian,
Jewish or, later, Islamic belief. In many cases this strand of early
Christian writing makes for fairly dull reading fifteen centuries or
so later.

Meanwhile, Augustine gave a genuinely fascinating account of
his life in *The Confessions,* which is an important book in many
respects, not least in that it is regarded as one of the first true
autobiographies, in the modern sense. The picture he paints of
himself is not flattering – he was tempted into evil ways and
pleasures of the flesh, was a follower of Manichaenism (a belief

system that was based on a duality of good versus evil) and strug-gled to achieve the ideal of chastity. A turning point came when he picked up a Bible and read a passage from St Paul concerning licentiousness, and this led on to his conversion.

Based on his own early life, Augustine saw mankind as weak in spirit, and only capable of gaining redemption though God's grace. He moved away from the Manichaen belief in evil, and came to define evil as the absence of good. This led him to regard rationality as being less important than faith in God. However he did still believe that philosophy can help us to understand our faith.

He rejected the sceptical belief that we can't know anything with certainty, pointing out that "Si fallor, sum" ("If I am mistaken, I exist") an early version of Descartes' later "I think therefore I am." And in a similar manner to Descartes, Augustine used this as the basis for asserting that we can have trust in our perceptions because we can trust in God.

In *The Confessions*, Augustine also wrote with subtlety and wisdom on questions such as necessary truth, and free will. He saw the latter as a function of the way that we experience time – God experiences the world without our limitations and knows all our choices. Whereas we have to work out our decisions within the constrictions of not knowing the future, and free will is an essential part of how we must live our lives.

In many respects, *City of God* is a more difficult read than *The Confessions*. He wrote it (in Latin) in the early part of the fifth century, following the sacking of Rome by Visigoths in 410 AD. This was a crisis point in the history of Rome – Christianity had been adopted, but many Romans believed that the sacking was a result of their having turned away from their earlier gods. Augustine's first aim in the book is to address this idea, by suggesting that it is not always necessary for the earthly rule of Christianity to triumph for the City of God to flourish. The book deals with issues such as martyrdom and the suffering of early Christians in this context, and analyzes the relationship between the Christian church and other religions, including Judaism and paganism. The full title of the book is sometimes given as *The City of God Against The Pagans*.

Christianity was by now the official religion of the Roman Empire. But Augustine is concerned with the idea that the fundamental Christian message is more spiritual than political. So we should look to heaven, rather than focusing on worldly events. In particular, Augustine asks us to contemplate the mystical heavenly city of New Jerusalem. This is a recurring theme in Jewish and Christian texts, the idea that Jerusalem would be literally or figuratively recreated in heavenly surroundings, a final destination for saints and the redeemed.

Augustine also focuses on the long sweep of human history in this book. He contrasts the City of Man with the City of God. Harking back to his *Confessions,* he sees the City of Man as being prone to weakness, licentiousness, and failure to recognize Christian values. Whereas the City of God (which is in his writing more of a metaphor than a literal place, even though it is sometimes identified with the true church) is made up of people who are able to resist temptations and devote themselves to the Christian message.

While these are the overall themes of *The City of God,* the book can be heavy going for a modern reader. Augustine makes many digressions in which he seeks to reject pagan beliefs on philosophical grounds, and this makes the book very much of its time. The book has also been criticized from a different point of view – some believe that it was a powerful influence within Christianity, but in a malign way.

This is because it helped to establish the idea that the Christian church was in a long-term battle against the pagan (or infidel) horde. This was obviously an idea that influenced the Crusaders and the Spanish Inquisition, and can still be perceived today in some of the extreme parts of modern Christian evangelism. It is questionable whether one can really blame Augustine for the excesses of some of those who followed him, but the confrontational nature of the book does tend to lend itself to such interpretations.

Overall, Augustine is a difficult but intriguing read. Part of the interest comes from the historical context in which we see the struggles of the early church to establish itself in people's hearts and minds in spite of political turmoil. But also there is inspiration to be taken from Augustine's personal determination to overcome temptation, and from his idea that the City of Man is ephemeral, while the eternal City of God is where we should fix our gaze.

City of God

The Speed Read

Pagans have wrecked the city of Rome, but do not be disheartened or return to false gods. What you see here is the City of Man, where people are often weak, licentious, and lacking in Christian values. What we are seeking to build is the City of God, where man's innate weakness is overcome through faith in God.

The Cloud of Unknowing, 1375 (approx.)
Anonymous

"God can be taken and held by love but not by thought."

THE CLOUD OF UNKNOWING is an anonymous 14th century spiritual guidebook. It is thought to have been written by an English monk (possibly a Carthusian). It is framed as advice to someone who is setting forth on a life of contemplation, as a young monk might be doing. It focuses on the idea that we can only approach God through love, not through knowledge and rational thought.

The author describes the human need to understand as a stumbling block on the route to reaching God through simple love. He writes that this need to understand will "replace the darkness which you have pierced to reach God with clear images of something which, however good, however beautiful, however Godlike, is not God."

It is a short text, made up of brief chapters, and it is surprisingly readable for a modern reader, in spite of the convoluted phraseology. It gives a good insight into medieval mysticism and the spiritual problems that faced a monk of the time, but it can also be read from a modern viewpoint – some have described it as giving a Zen-like view of Christianity.

The unknown author of *The Cloud of Unknowing* translated some other religious texts, including a version of the works of the fifth-century Syrian now known as Pseudo-Dionysius (or Dionysius the Areopagite). His work *Concerning Mystical Theology* took its starting point from St Paul's references in Acts 17 to "the unknown God."

From here he developed the system of belief that later theologians would classify as "apophatic mysticism." Perhaps it is unfortunate that such a daunting bit of theological jargon came to represent a way of thinking that is less complex than this label implies.

Pseudo-Dionysius taught that whatever image of God we might conceive of, the true nature of God lay beyond any concept we could hold in our mind. So he directed us towards an "imageless" approach to the divine being. Apophatic Mysticism is sometimes defined as dealing with knowledge of God that is gained from negation – this is true in so far as it is a belief system that negates any image of God we might have and insists that God is unknowable.

Instead this "negative" spirituality emphasizes the grand mystery of God, and the transcendence of rational thought that leaves God clouded in darkness to our rational minds. Other important writers such as Meister Eckhart and St John of the Cross would be influenced by this way of thinking but *The Cloud of Unknowing* is one of the most complete and eloquent medieval statements of apophatic mysticism.

Regarding the impossibility of knowledge of God, the author writes:

> . . . *thou hast brought me with thy question into that same darkness, and into that same cloud of unknowing, that I would thou wert in thyself. For of all other creatures and their works, yea, and of the works of God's self, may a man through grace have fullhead of knowing, and well he can think of them: but of God Himself can no man think.*

For this author, the fact that God cannot be reached through rational understanding means that we must recognize our own weakness in the face of the Divine. The voice of the teacher in the book varies between loving encouragement of the pupil and a harsher tone. In particular, when the author is emphasizing the humility we need to cultivate, he takes a strong tone of chastisement:

Look up now, weak wretch, and see what thou art. What art thou, and what hast thou merited, thus to be called of our Lord? What weary wretched heart, and sleeping in sloth, is that, the which is not wakened with the draught of this love and the voice of this calling.

However the teacher's aim is not to demoralize his pupil. It is merely to prepare him for the idea that, since God is unknowable, we can only approach God through unconditional love. He counsels that prayer should not be a matter of language or rational constructions. Instead, we should develop an "inner silence" – we should push all images and concepts out of our mind into a "cloud of forgetting." Then we should try with our whole heart simply to love God, even though God will always remain hidden from our conscious understanding by the "cloud of unknowing."

Here the author introduces one of the most fascinating aspects of his message. He counsels his pupil to pray by focusing on one single word such as "God" or "love," suggesting that by repeating this word one's heart can develop a love for God without the interference of our conscious rationality.

This is a technique that has been adapted by some modern theologians and some Trappist monks, in the idea of "centering prayer," through which a single word becomes the entire prayer. However, here we also see why some modern writers see a connection between *The Cloud of Unknowing* and Eastern religion, in both Zen Buddhism and the meditational practices of Hindu gurus.

Rather than encourage his pupil to conceptualize God, the teacher is advising him to reject extraneous thoughts, and to focus only on the love for God. But as we can't know God, we do not know what we are loving. All we can do is to try to send a "sharp dart" of love to attempt to pierce the cloud of unknowing:

And therefore, although it be good sometimes to think of the kindness and the worthiness of God in special, and although it be a light and a part of contemplation: nevertheless yet in this work it shall be cast down and covered with a cloud of forgetting. And thou

shalt step above it stalwartly, but Mistily, with a devout and a
pleasing stirring of love, and try for to pierce that darkness above
thee. And smite upon that thick cloud of unknowing with a sharp
dart of longing love.

The teacher can be a strict guide sometimes, as might be
expected from a medieval monastic viewpoint. However there is a
generosity and encouragement in the writing for anyone considering a contemplative existence. The author writes that it is "not
what you are nor what you have been that God sees with his all-
merciful eyes, but what you desire to be." So in spite of the
unknowability of God, the presumption is that as well as loving
God we are loved and forgiven by the divine being.

It is interesting to note that Apophatic Mysticism was in some
respects prefiguring elements of later philosophy with its emphasis
on the unknowability of God. The rationalist philosophers of the
renaissance, such as Descartes, would attempt to ground philosophy in certain knowledge derived from God. However Spinoza
and others recognized the impossibility of knowledge of God,
arguing that we could only work within the limits of our rationality.

Eventually Kant, in dividing the world into noumena and
phenomena, would argue that in trying to understand the
noumenal world (the world of things as they are rather than as we
perceive them) we inevitably come up against the "bounds of
reason." He argues that, as rational beings, we behave as though
we can have knowledge beyond the world we perceive, in order to
escape the intolerable possibility that life is meaningless.

Kierkegaard would seize on this idea and suggest that to
approach God we must make a "leap of faith." In each of these
thinkers one can hear a belated echo of the apophatic mystics'
conviction that God was unknowable, and that rational thought
could not allow us access to the Divine being.

The Cloud of Unknowing has inspired many mystical and contemplative thinkers over the centuries and today is still a very
readable and inspiring book. We may not know who the author

was, but their personality shines through in the text and the message is one that resonates in many surprising ways with modern thinking on spirituality.

The Cloud of Unknowing

The Speed Read

So you want me to teach you how to live the contemplative life? First you need to realize that you are a weak wretch, and that no image you hold in your mind can approach the mystery and majesty of God. So in a condition of utter humility you must try to remove rational thought from your prayers and, in order to approach an unknowable God, you must use the simplest prayer of your heart. Thus you will send sharp darts of love into the cloud of unknowing that surrounds God.

The Mirror of Simple Souls,
Fourteenth Century
Marguerite Porete

"God has nowhere to put his goodness, if not in me, no place to put himself entire, if not in me. And by this means I am the exemplar of salvation, and what is more, I am the salvation itself of every creature, and the glory of God."

THE STORY OF *The Mirror of Simple Souls* gives us a fascinating insight into the medieval church and the paths it might have taken. The book was written by Marguerite Porete, also known as Marguerite of Hainaut. It was written in Old French (whereas Latin was the approved language for religious texts of the period) while its author lived in an area which is in modern-day Belgium. As a result of the book, she was burned at the stake in 1310 after a trial in Paris for heresy. The book was burned, and only survived because of foreign translations, while it took until 1965 for careful scholarship to establish that Marguerite was indeed the author.

Why was this book so offensive to the church authorities of the period? Its full title was *The Mirror of the Simple Souls Who Are Annihilated and Remain Only in Will and Desire of Love* and it was a popular book before its suppression by the church. The title is a reference to the ecstatic annihilation a believer can find in God. It takes the form of a conversation in prose and poetry between personifications of love, reason, and the soul.

The book talks of the seven stages of spiritual growth one must go through on a journey to union with God. Incidentally, in this respect it bears a comparison with the later works *Dark Night of the Soul* by St John of the Cross, and *The Interior Castle* by St Teresa (both of which are summarized later in this book), which also take the reader through the metaphorical journey towards divinity.

For Marguerite, the noble soul is one that will resonate to the love of God. Souls resonate in the same way as bells, and some respond more clearly to the love of God than others. The path towards God is one in which the soul is eventually annihilated, in the sense that the soul no longer wills in a selfish way but wants only what God wants. In this union with the Divine, the self disappears, leaving only God.

This all seems simple enough but the church saw traces of the heresy of the free spirit in her writing and asked her to recant. She died refusing to withdraw her own words. She was accused at her trial of being a Beguine. In order to explain her accusation, we need to take a moment to explain what this means and what the heresy of the free spirit was.

In the thirteenth and fourteenth centuries, a tradition grew up in the Low Countries of Europe whereby individual women, not aligned to religious orders, chose to live a life of solitary prayer and contemplation. There were various influences on this choice, including the spread of Franciscan ideals, and the fact that many men departed on Crusades in this period. The Beguines were lay communities that grew out of this tradition. They were not nuns – they did not renounce property, and they took no vows. But they grouped together on the edges of towns and cared for the poor, living lives that in many respects were deeply simple and holy. A parallel movement of men, the Beghards also grew in this period.

The Beguines and the Beghards may or may not have been influenced by the Albigensians and Cathars, divergent branches of the church that had been suppressed by the Roman church. The main concerns for the official church were that they were not official organizations that could easily be absorbed and controlled, and the suspicion that they held antinomian beliefs – meaning that they felt that it was not necessary to hold to an established code of ethics that was legislated by a central authority. This worried the church as it felt the need to dictate its understanding of Jesus' teaching to its followers.

The church also detected elements of the heresy of the free spirit in the Beguines. This means that it felt they believed that it was possible to have a personal relationship with God rather than one which was directed through the intercession of the church. Obviously a great deal of the church's power in this period rested on its claim to be the sole channel to God, and the hierarchy was appalled by any suggestion that individuals could bypass the church at will.

The free spirit doctrine taught that through austerity and contemplation it was possible to achieve perfection and union with God in this world. This was characterized by the church as meaning that advocates of the free spirit ideas felt themselves beyond sin, although this seems to have been a willful misinterpretation of the real ideas being disseminated. Either way the heresy of the free spirit was something that the central authority of the church was keen to suppress.

It is not actually certain whether Marguerite Porete was a Beguine. At one point in her writing she lists them among her critics, and it may be that she was being falsely accused at her trial. But for the church authorities it would have been enough that her writing shared some elements of the same thinking, in particular the fact that it stressed a personal relationship with God.

So when *The Mirror of Simple Souls* started to be read and revered throughout France, the church reacted, and as was common at the time, it acted brutally to suppress the book. Marguerite Porete was burned in the Place de Greve in France in 1310 and the book would have been lost to posterity if the church had succeeded in its aim of destroying every copy.

Today, this is not an easy book to comprehend. It is poetical and uses some rather arcane language. Even when the language is simpler it is hard to unravel the references to popular and biblical ideas that are being made to. One needs an edition with a good introduction to make sense of the book if one is not a scholar of medieval spirituality.

However it can be an interesting read in spite of its difficulty, largely because it is a glimpse in the medieval period and into the kind of thinking that the church worked so hard to suppress. If the church had not been so diligent in crushing elements such as the Albigensians and the "heresy" of the free spirit, modern Christianity might look very different indeed. Certainly it would have a wider canon of classic works to draw on, and we are lucky that this one survived.

It is interesting also to note that the heresy of the free spirit went on to be associated with witchcraft in official church circles. Two fifteenth-century works, *Formicarius* by Johannes Nider and *Malleus Maleficarum* by Heinrich Kramer cemented the idea that this was a part of the belief system of witches. This provided part of the justification for the widespread witch burning which, together with the reign of the inquisition, did so much to damage the reputation of the church in the later middle ages.

At one stage Meister Eckhart was reputed to be an exponent of the heresy of the free spirit, but today his reputation is being rehabilitated in the Roman Catholic church. However Marguerite Porete has never been officially rehabilitated or pardoned for the "crime" of writing her poetic, spiritual work on oneness with God.

The Mirror of the Simple Souls

The Speed Read

An early fourteenth-century book, in which a debate takes place between love, reason, and the soul. It describes the seven stages of spiritual growth on the path to God, and the way in which a soul can resonate to the love of God. The eventual union with God is described as a kind of annihilation of the soul. The book was suppressed by the church, on the basis that it expressed the "heresy of the free spirit" and the author, Marguerite Porete was burned at the stake. It remains a glimpse into what the medieval church might have become if it had not been so determined to suppress all alternative interpretations of the message of Christ.

The Little Flowers of St Francis,
Fourteenth Century
Anonymous

"As our Lord Jesus Christ says in his Gospel, I know my sheep and mine know me, so the holy St Francis, like a good shepherd, knew, through divine revelation, all the merits and virtues of his companions, and also their defects and faults."

*T*HE LITTLE FLOWERS OF ST FRANCIS is one of the most enchanting, inspiring and downright funny spiritual texts one could ever hope to encounter. It was written in the fourteenth century, and was itself based on earlier texts about the life of St Francis. It has been credited to a Brother Ugolino, but in truth its authorship is uncertain.

The beauty of this little book is the way that it encapsulates the anarchic, humble nature of the early Franciscan movement. St Francis drew to him a motley crew of followers and this book gives a touching but unflinching account of some of their vagaries.

Everyone knows of St Francis as a gentle lover of animals, and as a saintly advocate of a life of simplicity and poverty. What is sometimes forgotten is the degree to which the ideals of the Franciscan movement challenged and undermined the church of its day. He was born in apporoximately 1181, the son of a wealthy cloth merchant. He had an artistic temperament as a young man, and one anecdote relates how he gave all his money to a beggar who asked him for alms in the marketplace.

Following a serious illness in 1203 and, apparently, a mystical vision of Jesus Christ, Francis became increasingly absorbed in religious contemplation. The turning point came when he heard a sermon in 1209 which was based on the passage from the Gospel of Matthew in which Christ asks his followers to go forth proclaiming the Kingdom of Heaven, taking no money or even shoes for their travels.

This inspired Francis to take up a new kind of monastic life in which he would travel in poverty and humility. He traveled barefoot around his native Umbrian region preaching, and within a year had gathered a group of followers, including the wealthy Brother Bernardo, who gave up a life of luxury, and donated all his money to the work of the emerging Franciscan movement.

They worked with lepers and the poor, the hungry and oppressed. But they not only worked with them, they joined with them and lived among them. St Francis also chose not to subject his followers to any kind of rules (beyond the requirements of their austere lifestyle) or hierarchy. Each Franciscan was free to make his own decisions about his actions, meaning that they practiced a form of anarchy within the movement.

After Francis traveled with his followers to Rome, Pope Innocent gave them the protection of the church. But on Francis' return to Assisi, the movement became increasingly popular to the point where the papacy started to see it as a revolutionary threat. One of his new followers was St Clare, who would later be remembered as the inspiration behind the Poor Clares.

Francis travelled to Egypt in 1219, where he put his non-violent principles into practice by preaching to the sultan about his view of Christianity. On his return he found that the Church had attempted to impose more standard monastic rules on his movement. This was the start of a long period during which the more revolutionary members of the Franciscan movement were gradually suppressed or sidelined by the church. After Francis' death in 1226, the Franciscan order would thus end up as a far less radical entity than it had been in its early days.

St Francis left behind a testament, and was also an early advocate of the radical idea that ordinary people should pray in their own language rather than the arcane Latin of the Catholic

Church. He always wrote in his native Umbrian himself. He was quickly beatified by the Church, and subsequent accounts of his life spread his fame, as well as distributing legends such as the accounts of him preaching to the birds, and taming the Wolf of Gubbio. But the most popular and enduring account of his life would be provided by the various versions of the *Little Flowers of St Francis*.

The title of the book gives the misleading impression of something light and fluffy. In fact the book is a collection of short chapters giving pithy accounts of events from the life of St Francis and his followers. Some of the events related seem simply absurd, others are quite beautiful. His sermon to the birds is given an eloquent description:

> *St Francis lifted up his eyes, and saw on some trees by the wayside a great multitude of birds; and being much surprised, he said to his companions, 'Wait for me here by the way, whilst I go and preach to my little sisters the birds'; and entering into the field, he began to preach to the birds which were on the ground, and suddenly all those also on the trees came round him, and all listened while St Francis preached to them, and did not fly away until he had given them his blessing.*

However some of the most remarkable moments in the book come from accounts of the exploits of St Francis' companions, in particular the frequently hilarious accounts of the activities of Brother Juniper.

Juniper is a strange figure, a devout, simple man who personifies the early Franciscan ideals, yet frequently behaves in a bizarre manner. One chapter of the book describes how, when a crowd approached him, impressed by his holiness, he proceeded to play see-saw with a child in order to abase himself and repel their admiration. On another occasion he takes lodging with some fellow Franciscans and ruins their entire week's supply of food by tipping it all into a single inedible stew.

In some cases there is a contemporary subtext to the Juniper stories. For instance his shortcomings as a cook showed up the fact that this particular group of Franciscans were not fully embracing St Francis' love of simplicity and poverty – and their response to his action reveals their discomfort in this knowledge. But regardless of the politics, the stories about Brother Juniper have a simple charm and humor that persists to this day.

Modern editions of *The Little Flowers of St Francis* date from a couple of centuries after St Francis' death when the current selection of stories first started to circulate. It was only translated into English quite late, in spite of having long been a popular favorite in Italy. Possibly the title implied a fluffier, less entertaining book, or perhaps it just took a while for anyone capable of translating it to come across it.

Either way, it is a valuable, light-hearted book. As well as being a very enjoyable read, it raises genuine questions about the meaning of Christ's exhortations to poverty and simplicity. The Catholic Church has always tended towards pomp and wealth, and the early Franciscan movement and its successors represent some of the few occasions when this tendency has been seriously challenged from within the church.

The Little Flowers of St Francis

The Speed Read

In this book are the Little Flowers of St Francis, meaning testimony concerning his miracles, pious examples of behavior and his teaching. St Francis drew to him at Assisi followers such as Brother Bernard, St Clare, and Brother Leo, to whom he once explained that perfect joy would be to accept all kinds of sufferings, impoverishments, and abasements in the name of one's love of

Christ. Brother Juniper took his love of abasement and poverty to such a degree that he often appeared absurd, yet even in his stories one can catch glimpses of genuine holiness.

Collected Works, Fourteenth Century
Meister Eckhart

"The eye with which I see God is the same eye with which
God sees me."

ECKHART VON HOCKHEIM was a German theologian and philosopher who was born in 1260 in Thuringia. Best known to posterity as Meister Eckhart, he was a well-known religious thinker who put forward some unusual ideas in a period when unorthodoxy was a dangerous thing. This was the period of the decadent Avignon Papacy, and a time when members of the Franciscan and Dominican Orders were often in antagonistic relations with one another. Eckhart joined the Dominicans as a young man, traveled Europe, and became a teacher in the Dominican schools.

The Dominicans were prominent representatives of the Thomist way of thinking – which simply means that they followed in the footsteps of Thomas Aquinas in trying to find ways to marry a rational system of thought to Christian basics. Eckhart was also known as a Neo-platonist – this was the section of the Church which attempted to interpret Christ's teaching in the light of Greek philosophy, in particular that of Plato, at least as it had been interpreted by influential figures such as Plotinus.

Part of Eckhart's writing is thus within the traditional scholastic tradition of rather dry theological debate. However he is a far more interesting figure in church history than this suggests. His thinking has a psychological angle, and he uses a fascinating range of metaphorical devices to communicate his beliefs. Writing of the mysteries of God's love he speaks of God's love as a fertile overflowing, and he talks about the spark of the soul, and the birth of the Word in the heart. Many of these metaphors convey ideas that are notably out of line with the church of his time.

He is also known for a series of sermons that he delivered in vernacular German, attempting to explain the mysteries of the Bible to ordinary people. A few centuries ahead of the Protestant schism, he was already concerned by the exclusivity of the church and sought to democratize by explaining the gospel in everyday language.

It is not then so surprising to discover that the church of his time found him an uncomfortable figure. He came under the scrutiny of the inquisition, which was by now largely under Franciscan control (something which would certainly have appalled its gentle founder, St Francis). Eckhart was eventually silenced by being tried for heresy in 1327.

He defended his beliefs, putting forward a defence that he had said nothing wrong. He said that in his sermons he had only meant to inspire in listeners the desire above all to do some good. It is unclear whether Eckhart died or disappeared as a result of his persecution, we only know that the trial marked the end of his public life.

Hilariously, a church decree was subsequently issued denouncing preachers such as Eckhart who "endeavor to preach subtle things which not only do (not) advance morals, but easily lead the people into error." Subtlety was not much appreciated in the medieval church, let alone giving the common people ideas "above their station." Eckhart's influence lived on in the Friends of God movement, but he is still a controversial figure in official Vatican circles.

So what did he actually say that was so problematic?

By the standards of his time, some of Eckhart's ideas were indeed revolutionary. He talked of how the individual soul had the capacity to become one with God, counseling the faithful to look inside themselves to find God. He talked of the human soul as being superior to the angels. He talked of passively emptying oneself of consciousness and allowing God to flow through us – and he talked about going "beyond God" to a still desert, a place where all things were created. These concepts sound closer to Lao Tzu's Taoism or to Buddhism than to the traditional Christian faith of the time.

For modern readers, Eckhart's sermons contain some fascinating ideas. One of his first concerns was to educate his listeners in how to search for God. He admonished people to look for God inside themselves, and suggested that they try to do this by finding a state of disinterestedness, or detachment. He talks of the birth of the Word, a kind of union with God which happens deep in our souls. He emphasizes that this alchemy can only happen if we are living a good Christian life. But he also stresses the importance of passivity in reaching this state.

By passivity or disinterestedness he is not suggesting we should be weak or negative. Instead, he asks us to place all the attributes of self and self-interest to one side and to allow God into our being. And if we can achieve this, he suggests that we can live with God inside us: "A man should accustom himself to having God present always in his disposition and his intention. Believe me, if you were constant in this way, no one could come between you and the God who is present to you."

So through this special kind of passivity, we experience the birth of the Word inside us. And how do we recognize this moment? "You must know that God is born in us when the mind is stilled and sense troubles us no longer."

For Eckhart, the spiritual life leads us to a condition where God is within us and in all things we notice only God. This sentiment has appealed to proponents of Eckhart's links with Eastern religion and to pantheists, but it is also a very specific interpretation of the Christian message, an individual one which was not welcomed by the church of his time.

Another way in which Eckhart's teaching was contrary to orthodoxy came in his attitude to monastic retreat. Following St Augustine, a large part of scholastic Christianity revolved around the theory that the ideal path to God was to retreat from the activities and distractions of everyday life and seek God in solitude. Thus the monks and priests of the church were granted a privileged relation with God because of their withdrawn role. But Eckhart acknowledges that we can't all live in retreat from the world, and emphasizes that even in ordinary life we can have God in our souls:

> *Whoever truly possesses God in the right way, possesses him in all places: on the street, in any company, as well as in a church or a remote place or in their cell. Grasping all things in a divine way and making of them something more than they are in themselves cannot be learned by taking flight, but rather we must learn to maintain an inner solitude regardless of where we are or who we are with.*

To the modern mind this is not such a surprising idea, but in an era when the priesthood was exalted, it was a very powerful thought, especially when allied with Eckhart's decision to preach in language that ordinary people could understand as well as writing his Latin theology.

Meister Eckhart was offering the church a big idea, when he suggested that the contemplative life was not innately better than the active life. He was putting religion at the center of our everyday lives, and suggesting that through a good life and through overcoming the self, we could have God in our hearts, whatever kind of life we lived. The church wasn't ready for his ideas, but they are inspiring to read, even eight centuries later.

Collected Works

The Speed Read

If we live a good Christian life, we can discover the birth of the Word inside ourselves. We must become passive and devoid of self-interest, and

then we will be able to find God in our souls. We
can do this whether we live an active or contemplative life, as not everyone can live in a monastery
or be a priest, but God can be in every individual.
When the word is born inside us, we will see God
in everything.

The Interior Castle, 1577
Teresa of Ávila

"I began to think of the soul as if it were a castle made of a single diamond or of very clear crystal, in which there are many rooms, just as in Heaven there are many mansions. Now if we think carefully over this, sisters, the soul of the righteous man is nothing but a paradise, in which, as God tells us, He takes His delight."

THERE ARE TWO different ways of seeing the life of Teresa of Ávila (also known as St Teresa of Jesus). On the one hand she was a determined reformer, who overcame considerable obstacles to set up the Discalced Carmelites, an austere branch of her order which went back to the basics of poverty and simplicity. On the other hand she was a mystic who experienced visions of Jesus and had a deeply passionate belief in her religion. It is impossible to understand her without reconciling these two separate aspects of her life.

Teresa was born in 1515 in Ávila, and first entered the Monastery of the Incarnation of the Carmelite nuns when she was 19 years old. She was a deeply religious child and was fascinated by the lives of the saints and martyrs. When she became a nun she suffered from a series of illnesses, but also experienced spiritual visions and moments of epiphany as she studied paths to God through the religious literature of her time.

After a two year period in which she experienced ongoing visions of Christ, she became determined to set up a new monastery in which she could put her personal vision of the religious life into practice. She felt that her contemporaries had allowed laxity into their practices, and wanted to obey Christ's strictures on poverty and simplicity in a more literal manner.

With the aid of wealthy backers she succeeded in this aim, setting up St Joseph's in 1562. She was a deeply controversial figure in the Carmelite movement and Catholic Church of her time, and faced serious opposition from those who didn't want her to succeed. But she was able to negotiate the difficult path to achieve her goals, along the way calling on the help of St John of the Cross and Anthony of Jesus, both of whom were strong supporters of her vision.

If this were all that we knew about Teresa, she would still be an interesting figure for her vision and determination in achieving so much in the face of many obstacles. However we are lucky to also have her writing to remember her by. She was a reluctant writer, only writing when told to by her spiritual supervisors. These included Fray Diego, her confessor, who apparently persuaded her to put pen to paper, but only after she received a vision from God giving her permission to do so. Teresa herself wrote of her reticence thus:

> *For the love of God, let me work at my spinning wheel and go to choir and perform the duties of the religious life, like the other sisters. I am not meant to write: I have neither the health nor the wits for it.*

She was so detached from her writing task that she never reread a word she had written. However we should be enduringly grateful to those who persuaded her to commit her inner life to paper. The *Life of St Teresa* is a fascinating book that records her life story and gives us a clear insight into her mind. But *The Interior Castle* is an inspiring book in a rather different way.

In her visions from God she found the starting point for her work:

> *A most beautiful crystal globe, made in the shape of a castle, and containing seven mansions, in the seventh and innermost of which*

was the King of Glory, in the greatest splendor, illuminating and beautifying them all. The nearer one got to the center, the stronger was the light; outside the palace limits everything was foul, dark and infested with toads, vipers and other venomous creatures.

She used this as a metaphor for the soul's journey of faith. She described the soul as a castle with a series of chambers, which could be compared to the seven heavens that were described in contemporary religious texts. Each chamber represented a step closer to God.

In these terms she describes the way that a soul progresses through prayer, leading an exemplary life, and on through an increasingly close relationship with God to a spiritual marriage with the divinity. As the soul progresses through these stages it increasingly withdraws from outside life into the interior castle and absorption with God.

She exhorts her readers to set foot on this journey, and to seek God. Like St John of the Cross's *Dark Night of the Soul*, there is something deeply passionate in the language she uses, describing the soul's search for God as being similar to that of a lover seeking their soulmate.

Throughout Teresa's writings there was a thread of mysticism centering on the ascent of the soul. She often talked of the journey that starts in contemplation and prayer, then leads to the subjugation of the will to God's will. She experienced many moments of spiritual ecstasy herself, and describes the ideal religious life in terms that include such passionate engagements with God. But one need not have her temperament to appreciate her descriptions of the soul's journey through life.

There is also an everyday simplicity in her descriptions of the act of praying. She writes that "mental prayer is nothing else than a close sharing between friends; it means taking time frequently to be alone with him who we know loves us."

This familiar relationship with her God is one of the aspects of her writing that make her so appealing to the reader. She manages to combine a mystical, slightly medieval view of religion with something very modern and simple in the way she talks of the daily devotions that are required for a religious life.

And somehow, in spite of the great humility her writing shows, her lively and engaging personality always shines through. We may not be able to take every step of the spiritual journey with her, but she is certainly a good companion to have on our own paths.

The Interior Castle

The Speed Read

There are seven mansions in the interior castle. In the first mansion, our souls are surrounded by sin, with prayer the only salvation. In the second and third mansions we find the practice of prayer and exemplary life. Through the fourth and fifth mansions we gradually give up our wills and do only as God wills. In the sixth mansion we pass from betrothal to a closer relationship with God. Finally we achieve perfect clarity and spiritual marriage to God in the seventh mansion.

Dark Night of the Soul,
Sixteenth Century
St John of the Cross

"What more do you want, o soul! And what else do you search for outside, when within yourself you possess your riches, delights, satisfaction and kingdom – your beloved whom you desire and seek?"

O NE OF SPAIN'S BEST loved poems is *Dark Night of the Soul* by St John of the Cross. It is a short poem that gives a mystical account of the soul leaving the body and reaching up towards its "beloved," God. Together with the commentaries written by its author, this is one of the most exquisite pieces of writing on the journey of the soul that can be imagined. To understand the context of this poem, it is necessary to know a little about the life of its author.

John was born in 1542, grew up in a village near to Ávila in Spain, and was initially called Juan de Yepes Alvarez. His father had come from a wealthy background, but was disowned when he married a weaver's daughter, John's mother. His family struggled with poverty after the death of his father and they were forced to move around Castile, eventually settling in Medina del Campo.

There he worked in the hospital with people who suffered from mental problems and incurable disease. The Society of Jesus (Jesuits) had recently been founded by St Ignatius Loyola, and the young John studied at one of their schools from the age of 16 to 20. At 21 he became a member of the Carmelite order, and studied philosophy and theology in Salamanca. Here he was taught by Fray Luis de Leon, who had translated the Song of Songs into Spanish.

This was an important encounter for John. The translation of biblical text in Spanish vernacular was still against church rules – because the church wanted to control how biblical information was transmitted to the common people. So this was a controversial translation, but also a deeply inspiring one as it brought John into direct contact with the great beauty of biblical poetry.

John intended to join the Carthusians, where he would have engaged in a life of solitary contemplation. However he came under the influence of Teresa of Ávila (Saint Teresa) and she asked him to help in her plans to reform the Carmelite order.

The two are remembered as founders of the Discalced Carmelites. Discalced means barefoot – in practice the Discalced Carmelites followed a devout, disciplined path, and reformed the relatively lax religious orders of the day. This was inevitably met with some opposition by their contemporaries who did not want to live a more austere religious life.

As a result of his reforming activities, John was imprisoned and tortured by his fellow Carmelites. In 1577 he was placed in confinement, and suffered the humiliation of regular public lashings. He was also kept in a tiny cell, where for nine months he suffered great deprivations. This was the place in which he started to compose the poetry for which he would later become famous.

Finally he managed to escape from his confinement and spent the rest of his life pursuing ambition of establishing the Discalced Carmelite order. His writings were not published until after his death in 1591.

Dark Night of the Soul is, along with *Spiritual Canticle,* his best known work. He also wrote a commentary to the poem, which helps to explain its metaphorical meaning and intentions. The first part of the poem speaks of how the senses are purified as the soul leaves the body in search of God. In the second part he describes the ten steps that the soul needs to take up a ladder of love, an idea which derives from St Thomas Aquinas.

The resulting poem reads almost like a love poem at times, as the delicate language describes the soul searching for its beloved, which is God. The poem also introduced the concept of the dark night of the soul into common usage. In essence this refers to the condition of despair that is felt by a believer who feels that his prayer is empty and unrewarding. While prayer can sometimes involve us in an experience of satisfaction and epiphany, there are times in the life of a religious person when they feel only an emptiness when they pray to God.

This can feel as though God has abandoned us or is refusing to listen. It can also lead us to confront our deepest doubts and uncertainties about our religion and beliefs. However the dark night of the soul is often a positive experience in the end. Instead of performing acts of virtue for the happy feelings they engender in us, we are left performing these spiritual acts for no immediate reward, only for the love of God.

Even while this love may feel unrequited, persisting in a life of virtue and prayer can lead us to a deeper understanding of that love, and we can recognize that we are acting purely from love of God, not from a disguised interest in self-satisfaction. Mother Teresa is one well known figure who went through a long dark night of the soul, but emerged from it with a deeper faith and happiness.

So in the end, the dark night of the soul can be a deeply spiritual experience, just as St John's long months in captivity led him on to greater belief and achievements in the remaining part of his life.

In the end John's poems have outlived him by centuries, and have been a source of great consolation and inspiration to many people, especially those who have suffered their own dark nights of the soul.

Dark Night of the Soul

The Speed Read

This beautiful poem describes a soul leaving the body, searching through the dark night for its beloved, climbing the "secret ladder" and eventually finding peace and abandonment with the beloved, God. But there is so much more to this poem that it somehow feels inappropriate to attempt to reduce it to a short summary, in spite of the brevity of the original text.

The Way of Christ, 1623
Jacob Boehme

"When Man will enter upon Repentance, and with his Prayers turn to God, he should, before he beginneth to pray, seriously consider the State of his own Soul."

JACOB BOEHME IS AN intriguing figure, a Christian mystic of the seventeenth century, whose thought influenced writers as varied as Angelus Silesius, William Blake, John Wesley, John Milton, and William Law. He was born to poor but devout Lutheran parents in 1575 in eastern Germany. He was always religious and concerned with issues such as the salvation of the soul. He also had many mystical visions. In particular he had an epiphany in 1600 when he was observing the beauty of a beam of sunlight and its reflection in a dish. He felt that he had had a glimpse in the spiritual structure of the world.

He was not able to devote himself to writing at this time. His work kept him busy, both as a shepherd and simultaneously as a shoemaker. But he set himself to studying scripture and to spiritual contemplation. He became somewhat melancholic in his studies, saying that:

> *I knew the Bible from beginning to end, but could find no consolation in Holy Writ; and my spirit, as if moving in a great storm, arose in God, carrying with it my whole heart, mind and will and wrestled with the love and mercy of God, that his blessing might descend upon me, that my mind might be illumined with his Holy Spirit, that I might understand his will and get rid of my sorrow . . .*

He started to write in 1612 and would eventually write 30 books. His first book, *Aurora*, set off a train of events in which Boehme would be persecuted and censored for his writing. A local pastor acquired a copy of the work and denounced it for heresy. For some time Boehme wrote no more, but eventually he was persuaded to start writing again.

The Way of Christ was his first printed book (previously his works had been circulated as handmade copies), published in 1623, and led to him being exiled to Dresden.

In the years after his death, Boehme's work gradually became more widely read. *The Way of Christ* is one of the most complete statements of his theology. He is strongly concerned with the problems of sin and redemption. Following Lutheran ideas, he wrote that mankind had fallen from a state of grace to the world of sin and misery.

He wrote of fallen angels who were on the side of evil. A more controversial aspect of his writing was the way he treated the Fall as a crucial part of the evolution of the universe. In his theology, man has to go through hell in order to reach God and a state of grace.

Thus for Boehme, mankind must depart from God and undergo conflict and suffering in order to make spiritual progress. He makes a comparison between a person's spiritual journey and the fall of Satan from heaven, and the inevitable separation of Adam and Eve from the Garden of Eden. He sees free will as central to man's existence. God seeks to interact with mankind, which is both part of his creation and a separate entity. Indeed, for Boehme, God is in some sense incomplete without the act of creation. By making the gift of free will to mankind he gives us the opportunity to find a new state of harmony.

This was one of the respects in which he departed severely from Lutheran teachings – the idea that God might be imperfect or in some way incomplete without mankind was seen as heretical. Boehme also departed from his church by emphasizing the need for self-awareness and faith rather than blindly following dogma. As so often, the latter suggestion was something that caused offence to the Church, who were striving to impose orthodoxy on their followers.

It is important to remember that Boehme's writing is constantly informed by his mystical visions. The church of his time took issue with theological details of this vision, but it is perhaps better to take Boehme's writing as expressing poetical ideas about God's relationship with man as he saw it.

As well as inspiring a group of followers, who became known as Behmenists, his writing became influential amongst those who appreciated its theological and poetical depth. John Wesley suggested him as reading for his preachers, while the theologian William Law wrote that "Jacob Boehme was not a messenger of anything new in religion, but the mystery of all that was old and true in religion and nature, was opened up to him . . . the depth of the riches, both of the wisdom and knowledge of God."

Meanwhile the suggestions of mysticism and anti-authoritarianism in his work attracted followers as varied as William Blake and the later Theosophists.

The Way To Christ is not an easy read today. The text is dense and hard to understand at times. It consists of nine separate chapters or treatises, and Boehme intended it as a meditation guide. He regarded his work as being dictated by the Holy Spirit, which he also described as the principle of life.

His unique vision of the trinity as being constructed of fire and light and his obscure references to the role of Mary and her virginity can be hard to decipher on a casual read. But there is something fascinating and absorbing in his writing, and *The Way to Christ* is still a thought-provoking glimpse into the mind of a seventeenth-century mystic.

The Way of Christ

The Speed Read

A meditation guide, based on the mystical visions of a seventeenth-century mystic in the Lutheran tradition. Focusing on the problem of sin and redemption, Boehme suggests that mankind must suffer the hell of the ordinary world of suffering in order to travel back toward a state of grace with God.

The Pilgrim's Progress, 1678
John Bunyan

"If you have sinned, do not lie down without repentance, for the want of repentance after one has sinned makes the heart yet harder and harder."

THE FULL TITLE OF John Bunyan's classic work is *The Pilgrim's Progress from This World to That Which Is to Come.* This is one of those books that is such an ingrained part of literary and spiritual culture that even those who haven't read it will be familiar with much of its content. The allegorical hazards and places encountered by the hero on his journey include the "Slough of Despond," the "Valley of the Shadow of Death," "Doubting Castle," "Enchanted Ground," and "Vanity Fair." All of these and many other phrases and names from the book have passed into popular usage in much the same way as phrases from biblical texts or Shakespeare have done.

Bunyan started to write the book while he was in prison in Bedfordshire in England. He had been sent there for contravening rules that prevented people from holding religious services other than within the official Church of England. Bunyan was himself a Protestant, but he was a Puritan, an independent opponent of the centralized version of the religion.

He had fought for the Parliamentary Army during the English Civil War and started writing the book in the later years of the Republican Government. The Puritans wanted the church to be purified, casting aside the remnants of Catholicism that had been retained by the Church of England. His writing showed signs of the revolutionary times he had lived through and he contrasted ideas of authoritarian government and law with the joy one can find through saving one's soul.

The plot of the book initially revolves around an everyman character called Christian, and his attempt to travel from the City of Destruction to the Celestial City. It uses a dreamlike narrative, involving strange encounters with other travelers and symbolic meetings with allegorical figures, to represent a soul's journey towards redemption. The book starts with Christian becoming weighed down by a terrible "burden" as he reads a religious text, and his realization that he must set out on his journey.

He is guided on his way by Evangelist, but is frequently sidetracked. First he makes the mistake of trying to relieve his burden through the law, on the advice of Mr Worldly Wiseman. But then a character called Good Will (who is later revealed as Jesus Christ) guides him on his way once again to the "place of deliverance." Here Christian is finally relieved of his burden as the straps breaking it come loose at the open sepulchre of Christ.

Following a battle with the mighty Appollyon in the Valley of Humiliation, Christian continues his journey through terrors such as the Valley of the Shadow of Death, and Doubting Castle, where he is imprisoned by the Giant Despair. At times he is accompanied by companions such as Hopeful and Faithful, although they gradually fall by the wayside.

One crucial turning point comes when Christian's courage returns to him after he hears the words of the 23rd Psalm: "Yea, though I walk through the valley of the shadow of death, I will fear no evil: for thou art with me; thy rod and thy staff they comfort me."

Finally Christian and Hopeful get beyond the Enchanted Ground to the Land of Beulah, then finally they cross the River of Death to reach Mount Zion and the Celestial City, where they are welcomed.

Bunyan also wrote a second part to the book, which is often published in a single volume with the first. In this one Christian's wife Christiana sets off on the same route as her husband with members of her family. In this case the journey is a longer one, one that more closely resembles a real life progress. The narrative focuses more on the everyday life of the pilgrims and emphasizes the joy of the pilgrimage itself as well as the struggles they go through on their path towards the Celestial City.

Bunyan's tone throughout *The Pilgrim's Progress* is often quite tough – his idea of how to live the holy life is a very specific one and some of the wayfarers who make mistakes are made to pay for their mistakes in a harsh manner. But at the same time the book has a kind of fairy tale appeal that makes it something that has been popular even with children. And certainly it is one of the most powerful and influential allegories of a soul's journey that has ever been written.

The book was hugely successful, being translated into more than 200 languages. It quickly reached the United States where it was widely read in the new Puritan communities. And to this day the book has always been in print somewhere in the world.

It also influenced many successors who either imitated its allegorical, dreamy style, or who found other ways to relate the journey of a soul through life. It has also been influential in a purely literary sense as many writers have either imitated or parodied its style, in particular in the names of the characters and places involved in Christian's journey. One can even see remnants of its influence in such disparate modern children's writers as Enid Blyton (who wrote her own version of the book, *The Land of Far Beyond*) and J.K. Rowling.

It is not always an easy or comforting read as its Christian message is a very specific, purist one, in keeping with Bunyan's Puritan beliefs. However it can be an inspiring read for both young and old, and can be described fairly as one of the most influential religious books in history.

The Pilgrim's Progress

The Speed Read

One day Christian realised he was carrying a heavy burden. He set off to relieve himself of this burden, making a difficult and danger-fraught journey. Along the way he encountered a series of people and places with allegorical names that identify their role. His journey was a metaphor for the Christian journey through life, toward redemption. Guided by, among others, Jesus Christ and Evangelist, he managed to rid himself of his burden, and to travel on to finally reach the Celestial City. Then his wife made the same journey but meeting even more fantastical characters along the way. Life is difficult and the way is narrow, but faith in Christ can save us in the end.

Later Christian Writings

Later Christian Writings: Introduction

THE LAST FEW centuries have been an age of great advances in science and rationalism. As a result, religion has at times seemed to be under threat from the growth of relativism and nihilism. So it is not surprising that some of the most interesting twentieth-century writings on Christianity are those that consider the underpinning of the religious age in the modern world.

The first book in this section, *The Way of A Pilgrim* is something of a throwback to a simpler age. The pilgrim's faith in God is inspiring and a reminder of simpler times. However it is a book that examines some of the most basic aspects of faith, and tries to establish an understanding of what it means to life a life devoted to God.

The other books included here are all from the twentieth and twenty-first centuries, and all address the basic problems of faith in the modern world. *Orthodoxy* by G.K. Chesterton is an interesting book because it makes an argument that one doesn't read too often, which is that we should defer to the authority of the church. Writers - even spiritual writers – tend to be individualists, so they are perhaps less likely than other people to wish to make the argument that we should conform to orthodoxy, but Chesterton makes an interesting argument for this point of view.

The Screwtape Letters is similarly focused on the essential problems of faith and temptation, but is a more humorous book. The works of Francis Schaeffer and Henry Nouwen each takes a look at the essential roots of Christian faith. Meanwhile Timothy Keller's 2008 book *The Reason for God* returns to the old-fashioned tradition of Christian apologetics. Keller looks at the arguments for scepticism and for rejecting Christianity and calmly debunks the certainty of the non-Christian position.

These titles are all ones that have their own value in an age when doubt and scepticism are rife. It could perhaps be said that the two great dangers of the modern world are excessively dogmatic religious movements and the forces of nihilism and faith-lessness. The task facing the modern believer is how to steer a reasonable path between these extremes.

The Way of a Pilgrim,
Nineteenth Century
Anonymous

*"My worldly goods are a knapsack and some dried bread in it,
and a Bible in my breast pocket. And that is all."*

IN I THESSALONIANS 5:17, St Paul gave believers a notoriously impossible command, when he exhorted them to "pray always." One response to this suggestion is given by the classic Russian work *The Way of A Pilgrim*. This is a charming book, about the author of which little is known. It is not even clear if it is an autobiographical account of the wandering of a hermit, or a well-constructed piece of spiritual fiction. But either way, the book has been instrumental in popularizing both the Jesus Prayer and the idea of silent prayer.

The book is squarely within the Orthodox Christian tradition, and takes its authority from the Orthodox text the *Philokalia*, in which the Greek Church Fathers advocated the idea of *hesychasm*. This is based on Christ's instruction in Matthew's gospel to "go into your closet and pray." In practice this involves turning inward to find a still center from which one can achieve a knowledge of God.

The specific method recommended in *The Way of A Pilgrim* involves repeating the Jesus prayer endlessly to oneself. Rather than getting bogged down in theological detail, the anonymous narrator chooses simply to start praying and to continue doing so. The *starets* (religious father) who teaches him how to use the prayer advises him to study the *Philokalia* and instructs him thus on the use of the Jesus Prayer:

Sit down in silence. Lower your head, shut your eyes, breathe out gently, and imagine yourself looking into your own heart. Carry your mind, that is, your thoughts, from your head to your heart. As you breathe out, say, "Lord Jesus Christ, have mercy on me." Say it moving your lips gently, or simply say it in your mind. Try to put all other thoughts aside. Be calm, be patient, and repeat the process very frequently.

The book is an account of the pilgrim's wanderings and his attempt to come to terms with the process of praying ceaselessly, as advised by the starets. One of the reasons for its popularity today is the engaging style of the narrator. He starts the book by telling us this about himself:

By the grace of God I am a Christian man, by my actions a great sinner, and by calling a homeless wanderer of the humblest birth who roams from place to place.

He proceeds to tell us of his travels and of the various sinners, drunks and homeless people he meets along the way. The pilgrim himself remains a cipher, or everyman, and we discover relatively little about him, not even his name. The small amount of information he gives about his family provide a few hints.

His parents died while he was young and he grew up with his grandfather and elder brother. The latter accidentally injured him in a rough game in their childhood, leaving him with a crippled left arm, meaning that he is unable to do much manual labor. The elder brother became an alcoholic. After the death of their grandfather, he burned down the house, which the younger brother now shared with his young wife, in a fit of jealousy. The wife ended up dying of a fever, leaving the pilgrim to wander the world alone.

The vision this narrative gives us of nineteenth-century Russia is one that rings true to anyone who is familiar with the novels of Dostoevsky or Tolstoy. Having heard of St Paul's admonition to constant prayer, he rejects the material world and sets out to discover how he can achieve this goal. This is the journey that leads him to the starets and the Jesus Prayer.

The book is divided into four sections, through which his travels and experiences develop. There is a sequel, *The Pilgrim Continues His Way*, which is often included with the first book in a single volume. The provenance of both books is in doubt, and some believe the second volume is written by a different person.

The books first came to light on Mount Athos, and many believe that the first book was written by a Russian traveler, while the second may have been a continuation of the work written by a Greek monk from the holy mountain. Certainly the ideas advocated in the book, of living as a hermit in simplicity and constant prayer would have been given an enthusiastic reception in the rarefied atmosphere of Mount Athos, although most readers judge the second book to be more dry and theoretical than the first. The author of the first book is clearly well-informed however, and refers to well known religious figures such as St. Simeon the New Theologian, Ignatius, Peter the Damascene, and, John Climaticus.

To start with, the pilgrim repeats the Jesus prayer 6,000 times a day, although he soon doubles this to 12,000. Eventually the prayer synchronizes with his breathing and walking to become natural part of his life. After working on a farm, he decides to travel to Siberia in search of greater silence. He walks 60 miles a day, begging for no more than dry bread, salt, and water from the villages and farms along the way. One of the interesting aspects of the book is the way that his life as a wanderer seems to play as strong a role in his developing understanding of spirituality as his use of ceaseless prayer.

Some of the pilgrim's encounters are especially charming. At one stage the children of a family accost him, calling him "Dear little beggar" and inviting him to their house, because their mother is so fond of beggars. The pilgrim stays with this family for a while, passing on what he has learned in a series of conversations.

However the pilgrim also encounters adversity. He is forced to fight off a wolf, and is jailed and flogged after an incident with a young woman – she was facing a forced marriage and the pilgrim advised her to flee. After she catches up with the pilgrim on the road, he teaches her about prayer, but the groom discovers them and the pilgrim is accused of seducing her away. The pilgrim describes such unfortunate incidents in a stoical tone that suggests he sees them merely lessons from God.

After his travels, the narrator ends the book by revealing that he has traveled to Kiev and is planning to move on to Jerusalem. It is not a long book, but he feels obliged to end with the self-effacing comment:

> *I have already chatted far too much. And the holy fathers call even spiritual talk mere babble if it lasts too long.*

The popularity of this sweet and profound little book was boosted when it was used by J.D. Salinger as a central part of the plot of *Franny and Zooey*. Part of its modern appeal comes from the fact that the wanderer's spirituality revolves partly around his travels, and the easy way he relates the incidents that happen to him on his journey.

Some modern readers have also related the idea of the Jesus Prayer to meditation, and the use of koans and mantras within Eastern religion, although the book also sits easily within the mainstream of Orthodox Christianity. It can be read as a simple theological introduction to ideas that can be pursued further by reading the *Philokalia*. But it can also be read as a profound meditation on silence, receptiveness, and inward prayer.

The Way of A Pilgrim

The Speed Read

After my miserable Russian childhood, I chose to wander the world, trying to discover what the Bible meant when it advised us to pray ceaselessly. A wise man told me how to approach the holy books, and also taught me to use the Jesus Prayer, "Lord Jesus Christ, have mercy on me," as a constant prayer. Through this prayer and my ongoing solitary wanderings, I came to a deeper understanding of spirituality and how prayer can lead us to God. Now I will continue my journey, but I have kept you for long enough.

Orthodoxy, 19th Century
G.K. Chesterton

*"This, therefore, is, in conclusion, my reason for accepting the religion
and not merely the scattered and secular truths out of the religion.
I do it because the thing has not merely told this truth or that truth,
but has revealed itself as a truth-telling thing. All other philosophers
say the things that plainly seem to be true; only this philosophy has
again and again said the thing that does not seem to be true, but is true."*

*O*RTHODOXY IS AN UNUSUAL book because it is a defence of a
very specific idea, that not only should we accept the
teaching of the church, but we should be prepared to
respect the specific authority of the church and accept that as
being superior to our own individual judgment. Many books
address problems of faith from a more individual viewpoint, but
not so many modern books specifically address the idea of subju-
gating ourselves to the church.

Chesterton, the English writer and journalist, wrote the book as
a companion to his earlier book *Heretics.* In the preface he explains
that he had decided to "attempt an explanation, not of whether
the Christian Faith can be believed, but of how he personally has
come to believe it." His views at this point were fairly specifically
Roman Catholic, and the book needs to be read with this in mind,
as part of his project is a defence of the Church's historical actions.

He describes Christianity as being a natural answer to human
needs, the solution to the problems we face, and a solution that is
naturally superior to other solutions. The book is based on autobiographical observations. As a metaphor for his spiritual search

Chesterton describes a man setting off from his hometown, traveling for many days, only to arrive back where he started. His point is that the man would now see his hometown through new, clearer eyes, and this is the viewpoint he hopes he is able to bring to the idea of Christianity.

To describe the book, it's necessary to briefly describe the logic of its argument. He starts by describing mankind's spiritual needs and proposing that Christianity might be a reasonable solution to those needs. To support this he takes some time to consider and dismiss some of the contemporary alternatives.

This section sees Chesterton at his most infuriating – his rejections of the ideas of pragmatism, evolution, enlightenment rationalism, and the continental ideas of thinkers such as Nietzsche and Schopenhauer are mostly based on, inadequate accounts of the actual ideas involved. At one stage he argues thus, in defence of the oppressive systems of past religious authorities:

> *The creeds and the crusades, the hierarchies and the horrible perse-cutions were not organized, as is ignorantly said, for the suppres-sion of reason. They were organized for the difficult defence of reason. Man, by a blind instinct, knew that if once things were wildly questioned, reason could be questioned first. The authority of priests to absolve, the authority of popes to define the authority, even of inquisitors to terrify: these were all only dark defences erected round one central authority, more undemonstrable, more supernatural than all – the authority of a man to think.*

As a defense of Christianity over rationalism, this is a very weak argument. Historically, it is clear that many parts of the church, including the inquisition, were indeed intent on the suppression of reason. And the failure to acknowledge this fatally undermines an argument that would otherwise be effective. This is unfortunate because Chesterton is here touching on some fascinating points – in particular the idea that the complete rejection of orthodox religion in favor of science and rationalism can lead to a nihilistic, relativistic void, into which new mythologies and authorities will step.

The rise of communism and fascism over the ensuing decades would bear out this analysis to some degree. A far more rigorous version of this argument would eventually be made in *The Dialectic of Enlightenment,* in which Max Horkheimer and Theodor Adorno argue that the apparent victory of subjective reason over objective reason as a result of the Enlightenment had in fact created a new and more dangerous age of myth, freed from the old certainties and faiths.

So the slackness of Chesterton's argument in these sections is disappointing. He fails to explain why a reasonable person should reject rationalism and science for Christianity. When it comes to evolution he argues that "if evolution simply means that a positive thing called an ape turned very slowly into a positive thing called a man, then it is stingless for the most orthodox; for a personal God might just as well do things slowly as quickly, especially if . . . he were outside time."

But rather than follow through on the promise of this argument he rejects the idea of evolution on the basis that he prefers to accept the orthodoxies of the church than to allow them to adapt to modern science. This may be one of the reasons why Chesterton's book is now popular with evangelical Christians and others who prefer to hold to a fundamentalist interpretation of Christianity rather than allow the church to grow and adapt to modern science.

Orthodoxy improves considerably when Chesterton moves on to talk about man's basic attitude to the world. He talks about how it is reasonable for us to view the world in wonder, to believe that it holds meaning, that it has been designed for a purpose, and to react to this idea with humility and respect. He goes on to consider the views of those who reject Christianity.

Again this section is somewhat flawed by rejections of opposing arguments that are rather too simplistic. Basically he argues that because people have attacked Christianity from a variety of opposing positions they can't all be right and there must be something peculiarly right about Chrsitianity. This of course isn't a logical argument, even though Chesterton makes his case in an engaging and appealing way.

Finally Chesterton moves on to a rather personal view of the structure of Christian thought and the reasons why he believes it to be the best and most reasonable answer to human spiritual needs. The book really comes alive in these passages, as Chesterton devotes more time to explaining his own faith.

He also talks engagingly about the reasons why we should accept the authority of the church. He talks about a child who learns to trust his father when they are told that, for instance, a flower will smell a certain way. He points out that the child need not come up with a complex scientific reason to trust their father, or to justify the parental authority with resort to psychology or other rationalisations.

They simply trust their father because he has always been the person they trust the most. They have found him to be someone who tells them the truth about the world so why wouldn't they trust him?

In sections such as these, Chesterton writes powerfully. And in the book as a whole there is an argument that almost succeeds. One can accept his overall thesis that the result of rationalism is for people to lose their faith in orthodoxy and that, as a result, we lose something valuable. But his argument is very idiosyncratic and personal and is unlikely to persuade anyone who doesn't share his specific beliefs.

This is a book that is enjoyable to read. Sometimes it provokes one to argue with the writer, other times to nod in agreement. It is probably not as good an apology for simple Christianity as *Mere Christianity* by C.S. Lewis, to which it is often compared. But it is an honest and interesting account of one writer's reasons for trusting in his church. As such it makes an interesting read for anyone who believes that it is important to respect some form of religious authority, whether that be a trusted preacher, the official Church, or simply the teaching that is passed down to us from our families.

Orthodoxy

The Speed Read

Mankind has certain spiritual needs and has to balance different aspects of their nature. Christianity is the best solution to this problem and something that any reasonable person could or should believe in. Enlightenment rationalism and science answer questions but don't satisfy the soul. Pragmatism, nihilism, and all the currently fashionable "isms" are piffle. People attack Christianity from different viewpoints, so they must all be wrong. In the end one trusts the church as one might trust a parent – because they have proven themselves to be the best path to truth and a good life.

The Screwtape Letters, 1942
C.S. Lewis

"Your man . . . doesn't think of doctrines as primarily 'true' or 'false,' but as 'academic' or 'practical,' 'outworn' or 'contemporary,' 'conventional' or 'ruthless.' Jargon, not argument, is your best ally in keeping him from the Church."

C.S. LEWIS IS ONE of the great popular writers on Christianity. In titles such as *Mere Christianity, The Problem of Pain,* and *Miracles,* he dealt succinctly but inspiringly with many of the basic problems and objections to the Christian faith. But one of his most entertaining books on the subject is a more humorous title, *The Screwtape Letters,* in which he takes the point of view of a devil in order to satirize and analyze the obstacles a believer must overcome.

Lewis had been baptized in the Church of Ireland, but drifted away from the church in his youth, feeling it to be a chore and irrelevant to his life. However he reconverted, joining the Anglican church, after a long struggle with his beliefs. Part of his inspiration came from his fascination with myth and history, in which his studies led him to conclude that there were certain ever-present themes in the human condition, themes that could only be dealt with in a moral way from the religious standpoint.

Today, C.S. Lewis is most famous for his children's books, *The Chronicles of Narnia,* which were published in the 1950s. The Narnia books often contain clear Christian messages, albeit in allegorical form. The figure of Aslan contains elements of God and Christ, and there are numerous storylines that revolve around faith, redemption, and forgiveness. Lewis preferred not to see the Christian content as "allegory" instead describing it as an imaginative recreation of what Christ might be like if there were a real world like Narnia where he underwent experiences such as those that Aslan faces.

The Narnia books retain great popularity and power to this day, even more so now they have been made into Hollywood films. But Lewis was already a well-known writer and broadcaster long before he started work on them. He made a series of wartime broadcasts on the subject of Christianity that made him a popular figure.

In his Christianity he was always careful to take a broad, non-sectarian approach. He didn't want to exclude any branch of the Christian church, believing that the broad message of Jesus was of far more importance than whether one chose to follow that message through the Quaker, Baptist, Roman Catholic, Anglican, or other route.

In *The Screwtape Letters,* Lewis chose a satirical form to convey his message. The book takes the form of a series of letters from the experienced demon Screwtape to the junior tempter Wormwood. Wormwood is in the process of attempting to win a human soul for the forces of evil, and to keep his man from discovering the road to God. Screwtape gives him humorous advice on how to achieve his goal, advice that centers on genuinely interesting questions of the problems of faith and belief.

Some of the humor in the book is rather broad – Hell's bureau-cracy is called the Lowerarchy, and Screwtape's references to "Our Father" and "the Adversary" are reversed from the usual Christian understanding of those terms. Lewis dealt with the problems and challenges that face doubters and believers at greater length in *Mere Christianity* and his partial autobiography *Surprised by Joy*. But the pithy and entertaining way that Screwtape deals with these problems from his demonic point of view makes Lewis' point as well if not better than those more sober books.

Screwtape often advises Wormwood on the usefulness of the "modern" point of view in befuddling the human mind. The many distractions that can be used to distract the man from God, the relativism, and belief in scientific solutions that can be used as justifications for rejecting faith – all of these are presented as the natural allies of the tempting demon. Lewis' own views are clear throughout, sometimes enlightened, sometimes a little fuddy-duddy and anti-modern, but always presented with the best intentions.

The book deals with sinful situations as varied as sex, love, pride, gluttony, and war. But some of the more interesting aspects of the book focus on the small everyday acts of pride, weakness, and selfishness that can turn us away from God just as effectively as the more obvious sins. Lewis presents self-interest and greed as human attributes that can be exploited by Wormwood to distract the man from the path of virtue and Godliness.

Throughout the book Wormwood seems a slightly hapless figure and many of his attempts at temptation backfire, to the impatience and irritation of his older mentor Screwtape. In the end the man's soul escapes Wormwood's clutches and he is left facing the inevitable wrath of "Our Father."

While it is a funny book in many ways, it is not one that Lewis enjoyed writing. He found it difficult and morally ambiguous to place himself in the role of Screwtape and to have to think about the world from the opposite viewpoint to his own. Lewis also went out of his way to point out that his use of demons as the main characters in this book did not imply that he believed in hell and demons in the old-fashioned sense.

He eventually resolved to stop writing the letters because of his unease about these issues, although he wrote one sequel, *Screwtape Proposes a Toast,* many years later, in which he dealt with what he saw as the evil of progressive education. This is one aspect in which Lewis' Christian writing can sometimes be tiresome – he can allow his political views to distract from the wider message, and thus to detract slightly from his more powerful messages. But this is a minor cavil about a writer who wrote some marvellously interesting and inspiring books about spirituality.

The message of *The Screwtape Letters* is one that is as relevant today as when it was written. For a vision of the small obstacles and temptations that can confuse and distract us from a spiritual path, it has rarely been bettered.

The Screwtape Letters

The Speed Read

My dear Wormwood,
As ever you are not making a terribly good job of distracting and befuddling your human patient, and keeping him from God. Follow my advice, focus on everyday weaknesses, pride, and self-interest, and steer him towards "modern" relativistic thinking, teach him to value "real life" over the life of the spirit, and you'll be halfway to saving his soul from heaven.

Your affectionate uncle, Screwtape.

True Spirituality, 1971
Francis A. Schaeffer

*"Christianity is not just a series of truths but Truth –
Truth about all of reality"*

F RANCIS SCHAEFFER is an intriguing figure in twentieth century Christianity. The basic facts about him can be stated fairly easily, but it is only in reading his work that the true complexity of his thinking emerges.

The first thing to note about Schaeffer is that he is credited with inspiring part of the modern activism of US right-wing evangelism, in particular its political opposition to abortion, and that this is partly based on his belief that the United States (and any Christian nation) should adhere to biblical principles rather than humanistic principles.

Secondly, one needs to mention the fact that Schaeffer is often associated with presuppositional apologetics. To briefly explain this term, there is a theological opposition between two viewpoints as to how one should approach the idea that God and scripture should hold primacy in one's thinking. Evidential apologetics follow Thomas Aquinas in attempting to find ways to demonstrate the existence of God, and the truth of his word, that rely only on facts that can be acknowledged by any rational human, whether they be Christian or not.

Presuppositional apologetics rejects this starting point. Instead it suggests that it is impossible to find such a neutral starting point, that the Christian worldview is the only coherent one and that any attempt to start from a neutral viewpoint is confused or contradictory.

Schaeffer certainly started from the idea that Christianity is true. But he did accept that a rational conversation could be had with a non-Christian – he felt that any non-Christian viewpoint was inherently contradictory but that this was because even those who rejected Christianity could not bring themselves to reject all that was clearly true, and that there was thus part of the Christian idea already in their thinking. Thus he saw it as the Christian apologist's job to expose the contradictions in other lines of thought, in order to demonstrate that Christianity was the one truth.

To some extent this all makes Schaeffer sound rather harsh and intolerant. However, he was writing from a fairly particular viewpoint, which was that society was becoming bogged down in relativism, modernism, and what he referred to as humanism – the idea that man is the measure of all things. His intention was to argue for a robust Christian response to those ideas that led to what he perceived as the negative and hopeless outlook of such modern theories as Marxism and existentialism.

In the 1940s the Schaeffer family moved from the United States to Switzerland, where he and his wife set up the L'Abri community, which still exists as a center of Christian thinking. This was a time when people were struggling to find meaning in the world after the horrors of the Second World War. Schaeffer personally went through something of a crisis of faith and a book such as *True Spirituality* should be read with the knowledge that it describes a personal progress more than it prescribes a path for others to follow.

It is an inspiring book in many respects, that describes how Schaeffer examined the roots of his own faith, came to the simple conclusion that Christianity is true, and made this realization the foundation stone for his life.

For Schaeffer, any attempt to comprehend the world without making Christ's message a starting point was doomed to flounder in confusion and contradiction. He saw the angst of contemporary political and philosophical ideologies as being inspired by a failure to recognize this truth. He had started out by studying philosophy himself, but felt that it failed to answer the important questions about life, death, and the spirit, and that he had only made any real progress towards understanding by reading the Bible.

It is also worth reading *True Spirituality* to get a more complex view of someone who has been taken up as a guru by some parts of modern Christianity. There are those evangelists who admire his call to personal action on issues he felt strongly about, while others have criticized him for encouraging the move toward a kind of modern theocracy as the ideal of Christianity.

Reading his own words, one sees more nuances than have been represented by some of those who followed in his footsteps. For a start he warned several times about the dangers of "wrapping Christianity in the American flag." This is a writer for whom the idea of personal conscience is of paramount importance.

He wants to persuade others to his point of view, which he believes is the only valid one, but he nonetheless recognizes the difficulties inherent in linking politics and religious conviction. Schaeffer believed in the First Amendment, guaranteeing freedom of religion for all, and rejected any serious step towards theocracy (the rule of religious law).

In a modern world where we perceive dangers both in the lack of faith and conviction of modern relativisms, and in the excess of certainty that fundamentalists of both Christian and non-Christian faiths evince, Schaeffer is a problematic read. But in the end he is a powerful voice that makes a case for religious certainty as a personal, moral choice. And *True Spirituality* is also a persuasive account of one man's spiritual journey.

True Spirituality

The Speed Read

The Bible and its message of salvation carry the "true truth." When we understand this we have a responsibility to demonstrate the falsehoods and inconsistencies of non-Christian belief systems. Christianity is not something we practice only in the church or in prayer, but something that is present in the truth and spirituality of our actions in everyday life, education, social policy, and business.

The Return of the Prodigal Son, 1971
Henri Nouwen

"Home is the center of my being where I can hear the voice that says: 'You are my Beloved, on you my favor rests' – the same voice that gave life to the first Adam and spoke to Jesus . . ."

THE WRITER HENRI NOUWEN (1932–1996) was a Catholic priest who wrote many books on spirituality that are popular with readers of different denominations. He was born in the Netherlands, but spent most of his life in the United States and Canada. In 1986 he left his life as a teacher at institutions such as Yale and Harvard to live at the L'Arche community near Toronto called "Daybreak," where he helped to care for mentally disabled people. He wrote a deeply moving book called *Adam: God's Beloved* about his friendship with a member of the community who suffered from severe disabilities.

One of his most fascinating books from a spiritual point view is *The Return of the Prodigal Son.* After an exhausting lecture tour of the United States, Nouwen was staying in a different L'Arche community in France in 1983. There he found himself contemplating a reproduction of Rembrandt's painting, which provided the name for his book. It was partly as a result of his meditations on this painting that he eventually chose to give up his lifestyle and take his place in the Canadian L'Arche community.

The interesting thing about his meditation on the painting and on the biblical story that inspired it is the way that he considers different perspectives within the narrative. In turn he identifies with the younger son, the elder son, and the father. In all his writings he emphasized the idea that we are all beloved sons and daughters of God. He takes this line of thought further by looking at each character in the story, and by pointing out that we are all capable of playing the different parts.

In the younger son, he identifies the part of us that wants to be loved and forgiven, even though we may not truly deserve to receive those blessings. In the elder son he see someone who is "doing everything right" but feels depressed that the love and forgiveness that he has "earned" are given freely to the younger son who has not deserved the same treatment as him.

Both of these characters' motivations are comprehensible. But Nouwen emphasizes that God's love and forgiveness are unconditional. The only character in the story who shows this is the father, and we all have it in us to emulate the father rather than either of the two sons. We are capable of expressing love and forgiveness in spite of the faults, pride, and weaknesses of others. The father is also the only truly happy figure in the story, because he is the one who is at spiritual peace.

In this sense, Nouwen is bringing out an aspect of the story that is not always obvious. Jesus is not only trying to teach us to accept God's love, as the prodigal son does once he realizes he is forgiven. If anything the moral of the story centers more on the father and the way that he offers unconditional love to the son. This is the example that Jesus would prefer us to follow.

The book also has a powerful message for those who are sometimes in the position of the elder son – feeling that they follow all the rules but are not appreciated. This part of the writing may have been informed by Nouwen's own personal circumstances. He struggled with depression at times in his life and also felt restricted by his role as a priest. It may or may not be relevant that he struggled with homosexual feelings in his life – meaning that as well as having to deal with the difficulties of abstinence, he found it hard to be honest about the exact way that those difficulties affected him.

There seems to be an echo of this in his sympathetic portrait of the depression felt by the elder son. And anyone who has been "good" and "dutiful" in their life may recognize the feeling that virtue is not always its own reward. However by focusing our attention on the father's example, Nouwen also shows a way to reach beyond this depression or perception, by seeking to emulate God in his unconditional love and forgiveness, rather than by seeking spiritual rewards for one's correct behavior.

In a later book, *Bread for the Journey,* Nouwen wrote this:

> *Although we tend to think about saints as holy and pious, and picture them with halos above their heads and ecstatic gazes, true saints are much more accessible. They are men and women like us, who live ordinary lives and struggle with ordinary problems. What makes them saints is their clear and unwavering focus on God and God's people.*

The point he is making so eloquently is that the holiest and most admirable people were not born as perfect paragons. They struggle with their own problems as we all do. And this understanding can inspire us to reach out and try to improve our own behavior and virtue, rather than making us feel inadequate. Nouwen's writing is inspiring for anyone who has ever struggled to live up to their own standards of spirituality as it reminds us that we are all only human, but can nonetheless aspire to become closer to God.

The Return of the Prodigal Son

The Speed Read

If one contemplates the story of the Prodigal Son, one can identify with the different characters in different ways. We can all be like the younger son – undeserving and living a bad life until we perceive the unconditional love of God. The elder son is interesting because he suffers from depression at the fact that his worthy behavior is rewarded no better than the wayward behavior of his younger sibling. Meanwhile the father shows us the model for how Jesus would want us to behave, because he shows unconditional love and forgiveness to both of his sons.

The Reason for God, 2008
Timothy Keller

*"During my nearly two decades in New York City,
I've had numerous opportunities to ask people, 'What is your
problem with Christianity? What troubles you the most about its
beliefs or how it is practiced?'"*

IMOTHY KELLER, the pastor at the Redeemer Presbyterian Church in New York City, has recently published his book *The Reason for God: Belief in an Age of Skepticism.* This is a defence and explanation of Christianity for the modern world, in the tradition of Christian apologetics that also includes books such as *Mere Christianity* by C.S. Lewis and *Orthodoxy* by G.K. Chesterton.

Writers have attempted to explain and justify their Christian beliefs from many different angles. Some have taken the view that one must attempt to prove the truth of Christianity from philosophical foundations. This was common among the early theologians (neo-platonists and others) who took a rather pedantic approach to the problem of proving the existence of God and such questions as how many angels fit on the head of a pin. In later centuries, philosophers approached the subject of religion from a different angle, with writers such as Descartes making God the center of a rational explanation of the universe. There are others who take the viewpoint that faith is its own reward and who feel that it is impossible and unnecessary to "prove" the existence of God when this fact should be the starting point from which we derive all our beliefs and values.

Timothy Keller comes at this fundamental problem from a Presbyterian background, but his approach to Christianity is essentially a broad one, in that he is addressing the basic problems of faith rather than the more detailed theological debates. In fact, one could argue that his work in New York City, where he preaches to a an audience that will regard itself as relatively cultured, sceptical and even cynical, provides the perfect background to writing a book of this sort. Keller patiently but powerfully looks at the arguments against Christianity that people tend to put forward and explains his own reasons for rejecting those arguments.

The book has been described as being for "sceptics and the believers who love them" and provides a blueprint for anyone who feels the need to defend their faith. He draws on secular material as varied as philosophical and literary classics and scientific accounts of anthropology to make his evangelical case.

Keller starts by observing that this is an age in which attitudes towards religion are becoming more polarized. He writes that "skepticism, fear, and anger toward traditional religion are growing in power and influence . . . But, at the same time, robust, orthodox belief in the traditional faiths is growing as well." As a result he decided to write a book addressing some of the fundamental issues in this argument.

Keller's approach is to address sceptics, and to ask them what the foundation is for their doubts. He argues that even sceptical doubts about religion are themselves based on assumptions and beliefs, and that by questioning those assumptions one can come to realize that the sceptical position is less certain than sceptics assume.

In the first half of the book, seven chapters address some of the most common objections to Christianity. For instance he deals with the ideas that a good God would not allow suffering, that the church has been responsible for great injustices, that science has superceded Christianity and that the Bible is mere myth, not the be taken literally.

In each case he calmly points out the assumptions that underlie the sceptical position and deconstructs them so as to show that they have their own difficulties and problems.

In the second half of the book he moves on to positive reasons to believe in God. He deals cogently and persuasively with issues such as the problem of sin. He also continues to insist that even those who deny "supernatural" explanations of the world have their own views of spiritual truth.

Some have questioned details of Keller's explanations of, for instance, evolution and his ecumenical approach in which he prefers to focus on broad issues of Christianity than to get bogged down in theological details. But one of the most powerful aspects of the book is the way that he addresses the whole issue of scepticism and shows that the sceptics make their own non-rational leaps of faith, just as they accuse believers of doing.

While we live in a world where both scepticism and faith seem to have increased in strength, much recent publishing has focused on the sceptical side of the argument. From Richard Dawkins to Christopher Hitchens there has been a stream of books that claim that all the problems of the world stem from religion and that the only answer is atheism.

Keller's book is a useful antidote to this tendency. He may not persuade every sceptical reader, and not all Christians will agree with some of his specific interpretations. In addition, he occasionally relies too much on arguments derived from Lewis' *Mere Christianity*. But the main line of his argument is a strong, robust defence of the Christian faith that will genuinely be of interest to non-believers as well as those who are already Christians, and which is ideally geared to the modern world.

The Reason for God

The Speed Read

In my church in New York, I've spent a lot of time discussing belief with sceptics. Here are some of the most common arguments I have come across against God, and here are my arguments as to why they are not convincing. Even sceptics are falling back on assumptions about spiritual truth, even when they claim to "believe in nothing." And there are many positive reasons for believing in God as well.

Approaches to Prayer

Approaches to Prayer: Introduction

ONE OF THE MOST basic practices of religious belief is prayer. We talk to God for many reasons – to plead for intercession, for daily comfort, for spiritual inspiration, and so on.

But how should we go about praying? Where should we start, and what is the best way of using prayer to develop a fuller spiritual existence? Should we set aside time for prayer on a daily basis, should we pray in church, or should we attempt to stay in constant contact with God? These are such obvious questions that we may sometimes forget to ask them.

This is one reason why the books in this section are of great appeal. Several of them, including John Baillie's *A Diary of Private Prayer* and Anthony Bloom's *Beginning to Pray* can be used as introductions to the art of praying. Bloom's book in particular is a marvelous examination of what is going on when we pray, and addresses questions such as "Why should we get upset if God doesn't seem to be listening to us, when we so often fail to heed his call?"

Madame Guyon's *A Short and Easy Method of Prayer* is a rather different work. Condemned as heretical in its own time, it is a passionate examination of our relationship with God. Like the anonymous author of *The Way of A Pilgrim,* Madame Guyon concludes that we must practice "constant prayer." Coming from a very different angle, Frank Laubach reaches a similar conclusion in *Letters By A Modern Mystic,* in which he takes a detailed look at how we might have God in our lives every moment of the day.

The remaining two books in this section, *A Testament of Devotion* by Thomas R. Kelly and *The Pursuit of God* by A.W. Tozer cover a wider range of topics, but they seem to belong here because, like the other books here, they focus on the very basics of our daily spiritual existence. Tozer subjects our religious foundations to an intense examination, while Kelly's approach is more meditative. However both books face up to one of the most difficult spiritual problems: how do we face up to complexities of modern existence and still keep room for God in our lives, indeed how do we make God the center of our daily existence.

The books in this section all offer different approaches to the problems of prayer and religious practice. Different readers will probably be drawn to different approaches, as the writers represented here have such different personalities. But each in their own way is trying to explain the most fundamental issues of how we should engage with God.

A Short and Easy Method of Prayer,
1685
Madame Guyon

*"May I hasten to say that the kind of prayer I am speaking of is not a prayer
that comes from YOUR MIND. It is a prayer that begins in
THE HEART ... PRAYER THAT COMES FROM THE
HEART IS NOT INTERRUPTED BY THINKING!"*

ADAME GUYON (1648–1717) is an intriguing mystic, a French widow whose book *A Short and Easy Method of Prayer* led to her imprisonment for seven years for heresy. The history of the Christian church is sadly full of cases where people's heartfelt beliefs or theories led to their persecution in the name of the prevailing orthodoxy of the time. It is always interesting to return to the actual ideas that caused such offence and examine what value they might have for us in the modern world.

In the case of Madame Guyon, the specific heresy was "Quietism". This was a form of Christian philosophy that was popular in Southern Europe in the seventeeth and eighteenth centuries. The Quietists believed that perfection could be achieved through a path of intellectual stillness and passivity. It was this emphasis on internal meditation rather than public duty that was largely to blame for the opposition of the Catholic church of the time. For a start, it was dangerously close to the Cathar or Albigensian idea that man could seek perfection and become sinless.

However Quietism has interesting precedents (for instance in Meister Eckhart and, arguably, in Eastern philosophy) and has had an enduring influence (to varying degrees) on thinkers as varied as Teresa of Ávila, Watchman Nee, the Moravians and Quakers, and even John Wesley.

Madame Guyon was widowed at the age of 28 after an unhappy marriage. She had been introduced to mystical ideas by Père Lacombe, a Barnabite priest. She moved from France to Annecy (in Switzerland) and renewed her acquainatance with him in the early 1680s. There she started to circulate her ideas. *A Short and Easy Method of Prayer* advocated constant prayer, and an approach to God which relied more on a passive heart than on the mind.

However back in France, she ran into opposition. Quietist ideas had been declared heretical and this was the start of a series of skirmishes and battles in which she would be forced to recant and withdraw her statements on various occasions. Over 300 copies of her books were burned by the authorities. Eventually, after a seven year imprisonment from 1695 to 1703, she withdrew from public life, choosing poetry as her only public means of expression.

However her followers continued to circulate her ideas and works. She had advised a life of constant prayer, in order that we might always be with God. Like the author of *Way of a Pilgrim*, she was fascinated by St Paul's advice to pray ceaselessly. She wrote that "prayer is the key of perfection and of sovereign happiness; it is the efficacious means of getting rid of all vices and of acquiring all virtues; for the way to become perfect is to live in the presence of God." In this pursuit she also advocated an inner stillness, a passivity that would allow one to become one with God.

One of the interesting, long-running disputes within Christianity is that regarding grace and works. Guyon (like St Augustine, St Thomas Aquinas, Calvin and others) believed that salvation could only come from God. She thus concluded that a state of grace was of more significance than holy works.

The danger she identifies is that those who perform good works in the belief that it will take them a step closer to heaven – in this case the action comes from pride, and a sense of entitlement rather than from true holiness. Thus Guyon concludes that even a wicked sinner, who submits passively to God, may achieve a state of grace that makes them spiritually preferable to someone who seeks the approval of God through their actions.

This is a difficult conundrum, one that goes to the heart of the problem of free will – because, if someone has free will then surely their actions define the choices they have made. Whereas if we are mere vessels of God's will, then all that can make us more or less spiritually pure is the grace and passivity with which we carry out the will of God. Madame Guyon's formulation of the problem may not satisfy modern readers, but it is an interesting reflection of a problem that still has relevance to believers today.

Another strain in Madame Guyon's writing that may not appeal today is the strain of anti-intellectualism that she shows. She writes:

> *Of course, there is a kind of reading the scripture for scholarship and for study – but not here. That studious kind of reading will not help you when it comes to matters that are divine.*

In a number of passages she seems to be advocating that the message we take from the Bible should be something that we instinctively sense rather than comprehending it with our rational minds. Of course the danger here is falling back into the kind of interpretive thinking shown by medieval scholasticism in which the bible becomes a web of "secret messages" which can be sensed but not rationally understood. In many cases it seems safe to assume that the meaning of the Bible is intended to be one that can be understood rationally rather than sensed instinctively.

One of the aspects of her writing that disturbed the Church authorities was the exact same thing that they had objected to in the much earlier work of Meister Eckhart. In a chapter entitled *The Ultimate Christian Attainment,* she writes that the final stage of prayer is union with God. Like many Christian mystics she talks of a ladder of prayer, and sees petitionary prayers as the most basic form of praying. For her, we must move beyond asking God for favors toward a state where we annihilate the self and become one with God.

Where the ladders of prayer described by St Teresa of Avila and St John of the Cross have a surface similarity, their mysticism stops short of allowing this possibility – for them God remains a separate, superior entity. The annihilation envisaged by Madame Guyon seems to have more in common with the declared goal of transcendental meditation than it does with standard Christian belief.

Nonetheless, there is much to fascinate and intrigue in the work of Madame Guyon, and as with other writers who were condemned, studying her can give us a broader understanding of the ways in which orthodoxies developed over the centuries, and of the branches of mysticism that were rejected.

A Short and Easy Method of Prayer

The Speed Read

Constant prayer is the path to perfection, because it is the best way to always be in the presence of God. When studying the scripture, you should sense the meaning with your heart rather than rationalizing it, and cultivate a quiet and passive mind. The ultimate goal of prayer is annihilation of the self and union with God.

A Diary of Private Prayer, 1936
John Baillie

*"Where deed of mine can help to make this world a better
place for men to live in, where word of mine can
cheer a despondent heart or brace a weak will, where prayer
of mine can serve the extension of Christ's kingdom,
there let me do and speak and pray."*

JOHN BAILLIE (1886–1960) was a minister in the Church of
Scotland and a well-known theologian. He was also a
professor at Edinburgh University. In his theological writing
he explored the way in which our experience of God affects
our spiritual lives. But he is best remembered for his book *A Diary
of Private Prayer.*

In essence this is a devotional, a collection of prayers. But there
have been many devotionals that are simply prayer collections, with
no great depth or significance. Baillie's book is a different matter. It
includes 31 morning and evening prayers, as well as extra prayers
for Sundays. The subjects of the prayers are extremely varied. Some
deal with personal confession, or with the spiritual life, while others
center on ideas about family and neighbors or about the state of the
world.

The prayers draw on a variety of source material, from ancient
prayers and Christian liturgies to biblical texts, though throughout
they are expressed through Baillie's own interpretation and style.
At times this style is slightly archaic:

Give me a stout heart to bear my own burdens. Give me a willing heart to bear the burdens of others. Give me a believing heart to cast all burdens upon Thee, O Lord.

The impression given is at times a slightly stiff, old-fashioned type of prayer. But the contents of the prayers are the real inspiration in this book. Baillie writes with honesty about the problems that assail a believer in daily life, and his prayers crystallize immense wisdom while being constantly thought-provoking.

One might not want to use these prayers as a blueprint for one's own prayer. They are too specific and too wordy to be used in that way. But they provide a wonderful model of prayer for those who might need inspiration or ideas for spiritual meditation.

One of the reasons this prayer book is so enduringly popular is the way that it deals with the mundane issues of everyday life. Baillie focuses on such issues as getting on with the neighbors, staying polite and civil, fulfilling one's daily duties, and keeping self-control.

He also focuses on the tendency to be tempted towards sin, and constructs the prayers in such a way that the reader can fill in their own weaknesses and sins. This means that the book also provokes a degree of soul-searching, in a way that the average cheerful devotional title does not.

This is a small book, but a powerful one. Baillie's love of God and desire to live a holy, spiritual life shines out from every page and provides an inspiration to the reader.

A Diary of Private Prayer

The Speed Read

Morning and evening prayers, with extra Sunday prayers for a month's worth of prayer. Much more than a standard devotional book, this book provides inspiration by giving an example of how one might choose to pray on a daily basis.

Letters by a Modern Mystic, 1937
Frank Laubach

"But why do I constantly harp upon this inner experience?
Because I feel convinced that for me and for you who read there
lie ahead undiscovered continents of spiritual living compared with
which we are infants in arms."

L ETTERS BY A MODERN MYSTIC is a collection of letters by Dr.
Frank Charles Laubach (1884–1970), who was writing
about the time he spent working as a Christian missionary
in the Phillipines in the 1930s. Laubach later became known as the
"Apostle to the Illiterates." This was because he was the founder
of the "Each One Teach One" literacy program, a scheme that
has been spread worldwide, teaching millions of people to read.
Laubach had a deep concern with alleviating poverty and
illiteracy as a tool toward spreading peace in the world, and in his
later years he achieved extraordinary results in his work with
Laubach Literacy.

However at the time that the letters in this book were written, this
was all still in the future. He was having a difficult time in his
missionary work in the Philippines. He hadn't yet mastered the
language and felt like an outsider, spurned by the locals, many of
whom were Muslims and were not particularly receptive to his help.

He spent a lot of time in contemplation of his religion and
resolved upon an experiment in prayer. He was thinking about the
passage in St Paul's letters to the Collosians which recommends
the virtues of constant prayer. He resolved to try to live his life in
constant contact with God.

This is an idea that had been approached in earlier works such as Brother Lawrence's *The Practice of the Presence of God*, a charming account of a seventeenth-century monk's attempt to walk in the constant presence of God, and *The Way of A Pilgrim* in which a Russian wanderer used the Jesus Prayer as a form of constant prayer.

Laubach brings a more twentieth-century, experimental approach to the subject. He writes frankly of his early difficulties in finding ways to live with God in the forefront of his thoughts at all times. But gradually he finds more success in his attempts. He writes thus:

> *Yesterday and today I have made a new adventure, which is not easy to express. I am feeling God in each movement, by an act of will – willing that He shall direct these fingers that now strike this typewriter – willing that He shall pour through my steps as I walk – willing that He shall direct my words as I speak, and my very jaws as I eat!*

Gradually as Laubach became more successful at keeping God in his mind at all times, he found that, while the effort of achieving this did not lessen, the other difficulties in his life started to feel far less problematic. He made significant progress in his missionary work, not only learning to speak the local language but also inventing a transcription method by which the local Moros could write down their words. This would be one of the starting points for his later literacy work.

In an age when it is often assumed that Christianity and Islam are opposing forces (largely because of increase in extreme fundamentalist approaches to both), it is noteworthy to see how Laubach approached the Muslim religion of the locals. While he always proclaimed himself a follower of Jesus, he was happy to study the Koran as well as the Bible, and to pray alongside the local Islamic elders. As a result of his tolerance, the local priests were happy to recommend his teachings on God to their followers. He became known as a Friend of Islam, and this helped him to spread his message.

In fact one could argue that his relationship with Islam went deeper than this. Traditional Islamic lore emphasizes the importance of submission to God, and this became a major part of Laubach's thinking, whether out of respect for, or healthy competition with his Islamic contacts. At one point he suggests approaching each moment in the day with these questions in one's mind: "What, Father, would you desire said? What, Father would you desire done this minute?"

Later in life Laubach would write the influential pamphlet "The Game With Minutes," in which he suggested that in order to keep God constantly in mind one should think of God for one second in every minute of the day. Of course this is just one of many approaches to the problem. In *Letters By A Modern Mystic,* he suggests that each person might want to experiment with different ways of keeping God in mind, since we all have specific circumstances and mindsets, and what works for one person might not work for another.

However one approaches the problem, the goal seems a worthy one in his writing. Laubach describes the state of mind achieved when one manages to concentrate on God as a peaceful state in which God permeates the soul and the world is transformed into one where, instead of individual striving, we seek only the will of God.

Perhaps the experiments described by Laubach go beyond the levels of devotion and concentration that most people can apply to their spiritual lives. But this is a deeply inspiring book. For some it will create the desire to follow in the path of Laubach, to experiment with various techniques for keeping constant touch with God. But even for those who do not feel able to go so far, it is a reminder that to make room for God in our daily lives, and a vivid example of the benefits that can accrue from doing this.

Letters By A Modern Mystic

The Speed Read

While engaged in missionary work in the Philippines, I decided to try to stay in constant touch with God. I experimented with different ways of achieving this, and gradually managed to make God a part of my life in every moment. As a result I find that "this concentration upon God is strenuous, but everything else has ceased to be so!"

A Testament of Devotion, 1941
Thomas R. Kelly

"Let me talk very intimately and very earnestly with you about Him who is dearer than life. Do you really want to live your lives, every moment of your lives, in His Presence?"

THOMAS KELLY WAS A Quaker mystic, teacher, and philosopher. The message of his finest work, *A Testament of Devotion,* is easier to understand if one has a basic knowledge both of the traditions of the Quaker movement and of his personal life.

Kelly was a respected college professor at Haverford College, a well-known Quaker school. On 17 January 1941, he reportedly told his wife that this was going to be the greatest day of his life. His elation was partly because he had just written to an editor at Harper and Brothers, a New York publishers, about a meeting to discuss the book he wanted to write on the subject of devotional practice. But this was to be the last day of Kelly's life. He collapsed with a massive heart attack that evening while drying the dishes, and died soon afterwards.

Kelly was 47 years old and had been developing a reputation as a thinker of note. Fortunately he was championed after his death by his good friend, the philosopher Douglas Steere, who carried on working on the planned publication. When it was issued, *A Testament of Devotion* consisted of five essays on devotional subjects, which were introduced with biographical notes that put the ideas into the context of Kelly's life.

Kelly was brought up in the Quaker faith in Ohio. Something

of a perfectionist, he was also a warm-hearted young man, interested in science, motorbikes, and carpentry as well as more spiritual pursuits. After studying at a variety of colleges, including Haverford, he trained as a missionary. He became a teacher who frequently had to move around the country in pursuit of work in difficult times – he was a young man during the First World War and his adult life was lived partly under the shadow of the Great Depression. He finally became established at Haverford College in 1936, succeeding D. Elton Trueblood in a chair of philosophy there.

At this time he was still studying for a PhD. It was in 1937 that his life went through a transformation. His dissertation had been well received but he had a disaster when he went to explain his work at an oral examination and suffered from a severe memory lapse. This seems to have been the trigger for a spiritual crisis in Kelly's life. Douglas Steere, who was also there for him as a friend in this difficult time, wrote this of Kelly:

> *He moved toward adequacy. A fissure in him seemed to close, cliffs caved in and filled up a chasm, and what was divided grew together within him. Science, scholarship, method remained good, but in a new setting . . . out of it seemed to come a whole new life orientation.*

In this period Kelly threw himself into a deeper examination of his relationship with God. The Quaker faith is notable for the degree to which it stresses the "inner light," and the individual's relationship with God. Rather than preaching dogma, Quakers believe that each individual must discover his own way to God.

The change in Kelly showed immediately in his teaching and way of life. He went to Germany in the summer of 1938, to support the Friends in a dark time in the history of that nation. He was clearly deeply moved by the suffering he saw there, but he was also going through a very direct experience of his faith: he wrote later that he had been "melted down by the love of God" in this period.

It was the teachings and writings that he created in the years between then and his tragically early death that built on his reputation, leading up to the offer of publication that sadly he would not live to see to completion.

A Testament of Devotion is a fascinating book, one that is not too burdened by theological jargon, although a passing knowledge of Quaker terminology is helpful in understanding it. Kelly writes of the ways in which ordinary people, living everyday lives, can search for that inner light that he saw so clearly. He writes in a gentle unhurried style about the complexity of modern life and the distractions that can keep us from discovering God.

For Kelly, the relationship with God is not a complex one that requires any great intellectual effort, but it must be one of absolute submission. He cautions us against looking for God in the external world, advising us instead to look inwards. He suggests that once we find God, the only thing we need to understand is how we can will the same thing as God wills. In another of his published writings, he says this:

> *Did you start the search for Him? He started you on the search for Him, and lovingly, anxiously, tenderly guides you to Himself... It is as St. Augustine says: He was within, and we mistakenly sought Him without. It isn't a matter of believing in the Inner Light, it is a matter of yielding your lives to Him.*

Kelly also writes penetratingly of the relationship between the individual and the church and his or her fellow seekers. He was gently critical of some of the secular tendencies he observed among his contemporaries in the Quakers, but he saw the religious community as having a supportive role in the life of the individual:

> *The disclosure of God normally brings the disclosure of the Fellowship . . . It is the holy matrix of 'the communion of the saints; the body of Christ which is His church' . . . Yet can one be surprised at being at home?*

From the day *A Testament of Devotion* was published it was widely acknowledged as a classic of spiritual writing. Throughout the five essays in the book, Kelly makes a compelling case for his view of God. He tells us to live our lives with God as the central point, to search for peace among the whirl and noise of modernity, and to find satisfaction in submission to God's will and in the spiritual journey that this entails.

A Testament of Devotion

The Speed Read

Modern life is complex, but rather than get drawn into looking for God in our external environment we need to find the peace to search within ourselves for the inner light. We must recognize the voice of God in ourselves, and aim to will whatever God wills. Life is a spiritual journey, a search for divinity, in the course of which we will find the satisfaction we crave.

The Pursuit of God, 1957
A. W. Tozer

*". . . it would seem that there is within each of us an enemy
which we tolerate at our peril. Jesus called it 'life' and 'self,'
or as we would say, the self-life. Its chief characteristic is its
possessiveness: the words 'gain' and 'profit' suggest this. To allow
this enemy to live is in the end to lose everything. To repudiate it
and give up all for Christ's sake is to lose nothing at last, but to
preserve everything unto life eternal."*

THERE ARE SOME books which bring us back to the absolute basics of the religious life. *The Pursuit of God* by A.W. Tozer is one such book. The author's engagement with the simple problems of prayer and a simple life are a reminder to us to examine the foundations of our own belief, whether or not we agree with every part of his argument.

Tozer was a Protestant pastor from Pennsylvania, who converted to Christianity in his late teens and became a minister in his twenties. He spent many years as a pastor and spent much of his life campaigning for a return to simplicity in the church, and opposing what he saw as the dangerous drift towards worldliness in modern religion.

In his own life, he chose a path of great austerity and simplicity, even once he had become a well-known and successful author. He donated most of his royalties to worthy causes, never owned a car, preferring to use public transport, and his family lived a simple life, reflecting his views on the message of the bible.

He wrote many books, but *The Pursuit of God* is one his best-loved works. He composed most of it in the course of a train trip from Chicago to Texas, in a single burst of inspiration. According to some accounts, much of it was written while he was on his knees, praying for guidance from God. In spite of the speed of its creation, this went on to become his most popular book, selling over a million copies and being translated into many languages.

One key aspect of Tozer's thought was his focus on the basics, such as how to pray. He had a strong belief that one could find God through the simple practice of prayer methods. He was fascinated by the Christian mystics and saw their devotion to daily worship as an inspiration to all. He would personally often pray sprawled face down on his study floor, in order to find the total detachment necessary to work towards a true spiritual experience.

In his writing he doesn't try to tell the reader to copy his example, but he subjects the reader to an interrogation concerning their commitment to the teachings of the bible. He accepts that we all have our own paths to God, and recognizes that a pure way of seeking goodness is valid, no matter how varied our paths may be.

The book is an inspiring read as it takes various elements of the spiritual life one by one and gives Tozer's robust, fundamental account of their meaning. In each chapter he looks at a different aspect of the search for and desire for God in our lives. With a few simple quotes, and a concluding prayer he outlines his views and urges us to remain steadfast in our beliefs and faith.

One difficult aspect of the book lies in its language. Tozer comes across as something of an autodidact and uses some fairly arcane theological language. Words and phrases such as *adamic, hymnody,* and *summun bonum* can force one to resort to the dictionary on a regular basis to try and interpret his meaning.

In general though, Tozer's focus is on a very simple point. He argues that at the heart of all religious experience is our personal relationship with God and with the word of God. Thus we must devote ourselves to the best of our ability to prayer and contemplation, and we must seek to learn to live better lives from our study of the Bible and the word of God. For such simple and refreshing insights into the spiritual life, this is a book that can provide much inspiration.

The Pursuit of God

The Speed Read

My aim is to help people in their search for God. I don't claim to be saying anything new, only to be interpreting ancient truths in the hope of helping others who are seeking for God.

"Others before me have gone much farther into these holy mysteries than I have done, but if my fire is not large it is yet real, and there may be those who can light their candle at its flame."

Beginning to Pray, 1970
Anthony Bloom

"First of all it is very important to remember that prayer is an encounter and a relationship, a relationship which is deep, and this relationship cannot be forced either on us or on God."

ANTHONY BLOOM WAS a well respected archbishop in the Russian Orthodox Church in the United Kingdom. This short book, which was published in 1970, first had the title *School for Prayer.* In many ways this was the perfect title for the book. While acknowledging that we are all beginners together when it comes to our search for God, Bloom is a wise man who offers some very basic advice on how to approach prayer. It's surprising that there aren't more books on how to pray, possibly because it seems like such a basic topic, but this book is invaluable for its simple approach to the problem.

In recent editions, the book starts with an interview with Bloom, who was also a popular broadcaster. This provides valuable additional information as it gives us a picture of the man who is the author, although one wonders if it would have been better added as an appendix at the end of the book.

The original book gets going with chapter one, *The Absence of God.* In itself this chapter provides a huge amount of food for thought. Bloom focuses on the relationship we are in with God when we pray. He acknowledges that all prayer is in some sense a moment of crisis. We pray because we are in crisis, or we risk putting ourselves in crisis by asking God to pass judgment upon us. And this means that we may receive either condemnation or salvation as a result.

He talks persuasively, but kindly, of the Old Testament idea that to be in the presence of God is a terrible thing. By this he means that when we place ourselves before God we have no defences left and are revealed as we truly are, and this can be an uncomfortable experience.

In talking about the absence of God, he is referring to the feeling we sometimes have that God is not listening to us when we pray. He gently reminds us that our relationship with God is an uneven one, and there are many times when God may feel that we are shunning him, and not listening to his voice – so what right do we have to complain if we sometimes feel that he is in turn failing to listen to us?

> *If you look at the relationship (us and God) in terms of mutual relationship, you would see that God could complain about us a great deal more than we about Him. We complain that He does make Himself present to us for a few minutes we reserve for Him, but what about the twenty-three and half hours during which God may be knocking at our door and we answer 'I am busy . . .*

So when we pray, we are sending messages into the unknown with no certainty that God is listening. And this is only natural from Bloom's point of view. To imagine anything else would be presumptuous of us.

He recommends the virtues of silence and peace as a prelude and accompaniment to times of prayer, and discusses what kind of prayers might suit us. Clearly different avenues of prayer will suit different people. One person might choose a personal appeal to God, another might focus on a repetitive prayer such as the Jesus Prayer, while another might choose to focus on working their way through the psalms as a mode of prayer.

The book discusses ways in which we might experiment with different types of prayer to find out what works for us, and this is one of the most valuable contributions it makes in terms of teaching us how to pray. It can be hard to face up to the fact that we don't always know how to pray, but Bloom is a patient teacher who does not make one feel bad for one's weaknesses in this respect.

For Bloom, the most important thing is to keep praying and not to allow the distractions and difficulties of regular prayer to prevent us from doing so. Crises in our life can become excuses to avoid praying, whereas those are the times when we most need to keep the conversation with God going.

He takes up a whole chapter discussing how we might best manage our time so as to make sure that we are always able to continue with our practice of prayer. And he emphasizes the importance of praying wholeheartedly, and with an appropriate degree of seriousness at all times.

In the later stages of the book, he focuses more closely on our personal relationship with God. He criticizes any attempt to have a functional relationship with God, where we see God as serving a purpose for us. Instead he urges us to get to know God on a personal basis and to have a direct, intense relationship with Him.

In the end Bloom is making the point that if we are hoping that God will listen to us, the only way to move towards achieving that ambition is to pray sincerely and with all our hearts. And if we are not sure how to go about doing that, there is no better place to start than this book.

Beginning to Pray

The Speed Read

Sometimes we feel that God is not listening to us. But on the other hand, how often can we say that we are truly listening to God? If we want to have a real relationship with God we must learn how to pray. This may mean experimenting with different

approaches to prayer. The crucial thing is to learn
how to set aside silent time in which we can pray
wholeheartedly to God.

Meditations &
Praise of Solitude

Meditations & Praise of Solitude: Introduction

I N THIS SECTION of the book we start to move away from formal religious doctrines and ideas into a broader spiritual realm. Some of these books are from specifically Christian backgrounds, while some (such as *Walden by* Henry David Thoreau or *One Day in the Life of Ivan Denisovich* by Aleksandr Solzenhitzyn) are not formally religious works at all. What all of these books share is that they deal with basic spiritual needs.

Kierkegaard is one of the writers here who is writing from a Christian viewpoint. *Purity of Heart Is to Will One Thing* is a book that addresses our relationship with God directly. However Kierkegaard's writing in general also represents an intense attempt to come to grips with the whole question of spiritual faith, coming to the conclusion that the religious life always involves a "leap of faith" but that it is necessary for us to be brave enough to make that leap.

Walden and, Catherine de Hueck Doherty's *Poustinia* are both books that examine the idea of solitude and retreat from the world from a spiritual angle. In each case the simplicity of life in retreat is put forward as a way to find peace and to advance one's spiritual condition. *One Day in the Life of Ivan Denisovich* is a rather different book as it is a study of someone in forced captivity where the simplicity of their existence is a punishing one. However it also draws out the way in which we can find meaning in tiny blessings, and also incidentally reminds us how lucky many of us are in our lives to be blessed with relative prosperity and security.

Gravity and Grace by Simone Weil is also an examination of spiritual suffering, in which the author examines our relationship with God and reminds us that Jesus always empathized with those who suffered the most in life. It represents a passionate reminder to look beyond our own lives in our spiritual pursuits.

In a different way, this is the message of *Leaves from the Notebook of a Tamed Cynic* by Karl Paul Reinhold Niebuhr. Niebuhr was a well known theologian who covered a range of subjects in his writing. But this early book deals with his experiences of living as a young preacher in Detroit. With humility and wisdom it points us toward the degree to which spirituality can be a communal experience. Niebuhr learns as much from his congregation as he can teach them, and is led by this to contemplate the degree to which we are all interconnected.

Collectively these books make up a series of meditations on the spiritual life that is grounded in religion, but that reaches beyond orthodoxy to aspects of the common human experience.

Purity of Heart Is to Will One Thing,
1846
Søren Kierkegaard

*"What kind of life do you live, do you will only one thing,
and what is this one thing?"*

K IERKEGAARD WAS A Danish philosopher who wrote in an intense and perceptive way about problems of faith and the individual. He can be difficult to read, but he is very rewarding to study as he is such a clear, unflinching thinker. He faces up honestly to the difficulties of a religious life, but by doing so he puts them into context.

He was an outwardly gregarious man who suffered from depression. He had a difficult childhood and a father who had turned against God as a result of misfortune. This may have contributed to Kirkegaard's intense reading of biblical stories such as the *Book of Job* and the story of Abraham and Isaac.

He used the latter as an example of a key concept, "the leap of faith" in his book *Fear and Trembling*. Like most of his philosophical books, he wrote this under a pseudonym. In his philosophical writing he often spoke of the *angst* (existential anxiety) we feel when we are confronted by the borders of reason (a term that had been used by the philosopher Kant to describe the limits of our knowledge, the point at which we confront the unknowable). This is the point at which an individual is confronted with, and terrified by, the prospect of their own freedom.

Kierkegaard identified three ways that people cope with the condition of human life. The aesthetic life is one in which we live for the moment, and hold beauty and aesthetic truth as our guiding principles. The ethical life is one in which we seek to live in accordance with rationally deduced moral truths. Kierkegaard sees either of these ways of life as incomplete – they cannot be rationally justified, and they ultimately fail to satisfy our wills.

He proposes the third way, the religious life as the only alternative. He is incredibly honest in facing the fact that the religious life cannot be justified on grounds of "objective truth". Instead he sees us as having to live our lives in a condition of "subjective truth", and suggests we must make that "leap of faith" to live a good life.

Thus Abraham's acceptance of God's instruction to take his son Isaac's life is analyzed by Kierkegaard as a moment when Abraham's subjective truth and faith forced him to make an apparently irrational choice. Kierkegaard transforms this unsettling story (why would God want Abraham to kill his son?) into a metaphor of faith. He also forensically describes the "fear and trembling" that an individual feels when he or she is forced to make that leap of faith and to embrace his or her own freedom.

So this is Kierkegaard's starting point when it comes to the idea of faith. But during a period of intense creativity between 1842 and 1848, he also wrote a series of "Edifying Addresses" under his own name. These are basically extended sermons in which he expanded upon his ideas of Christian faith in far more detail. One of the most fascinating of these is *Purity of Heart Is to Will One Thing*.

In this text, Kierkegaard confronts two questions. The first is "What kind of life do you live, do you will only one thing, and what is this one thing?" – while the second is "Do you live in such a way that you are conscious of being an individual?"

To explain these questions, we need to start by looking at Kierkegaard's ideas about the mass and the individual. He violently rejected any form of thinking that detracted from personal responsibility, and sees the mass or the crowd as something in which individual can hide from that responsibility. His entire drive in this sermon is to force the individual to confront their own weaknesses and evasions and to bring them in front of

God, alone and undefended, to face up to their own freedom. He talks of how badly individuals can behave en masse:

> *Take the highest of all, think of Christ – and think of the whole human race, all that have been born and will be born. Now the situation is one where Christ is alone, so that someone as an individual alone with Christ stepped up to Him and spat upon Him: the man was never born and will never be born, who possesses the courage or the audacity to do this: that is the truth. As they became a crowd, however, they had the courage to do it – oh, terrible falsity.*

So Kierkegaard labors to remind us that in the perspective of eternity, and in the eyes of God, we are individuals, not members of a crowd. In this he is rejecting the philosophy of Hegel who had spoken of individuals as less significant than the "world-spirit," but he is also making a deeper religious point. He was disappointed by Protestantism's failure to break more fully with Catholicism – he despised the organized Danish church for its cosy, political comforts, and felt that man's relationship with God must be an intensely personal one.

He also addresses Christ's comments that we should love our neighbor. He points out that Christ never advised us to love men en masse – only to love them as individuals. We are not equal, we have very different attributes and weaknesses.

The only level on which we are equal, in Kierkegaard's view, is in our relationship to God, in which we are all as children to a parent. And we owe each other love on an individual basis: "That one shall honor each individual man, without exception, each man: that is truth and is reverence and is neighbor-love."

Kierkegaard lived a life of some physical suffering, and was driven by a vocation to write, often spending his entire waking hours on his work. He neither embraces nor ignores his sufferings in his writing. Instead he interprets them for us in a revealing way. He acknowledges that his individual relationship to God is not for all. Instead he continually challenges the reader to study their own life.

He dialectically examines the idea of "willing the good." He argues that the only way we can "will one thing" without being "double-minded" is to will good without evasions, and without keeping back one little bit of selfishness for our own comfort.

For Kierkegaard, only someone who is "conscious of themselves as an individual" can truly will one thing in this way. We have to come before God as individuals, stripped of all our defences and evasions, and we must decide what it is that is our vocation. How can we single-mindedly will the good, how can we use our faith to live a good life in the eyes of God. And this life must be one that we can defend as individuals who live a life of faith.

Kierkegaard is simultaneously terrifying and exhilarating to read. He allows his reader no excuses, no evasions, and his forensic examination of his own faults leads us to contemplate how often we live lives of bad faith. He forces us to consider our individual relationship to God. One can argue with his writing – his views on faith sometimes suggest that a passionate faith in something false or immoral would be better than a lukewarm faith in truth and goodness. And one can question whether every individual need a life of such absolute vocation as Kierkegaard depicts.

He is also a notoriously hard writer to understand at first. Some of his books are very dense and complicated. But *Purity of Heart Is to Will One Thing* makes a surprisingly good introduction to his work. Here he is simply making the case for his very passionate and individual type of Christianity. One can agree or disagree with his conclusions, but either way he is a deeply inspiring thinker who challenges us to question the very foundations of our faith and relationship with God.

Purity of the Heart Is to Will One Thing

The Speed Read

If we can will one thing, then we must will the Good, for the Good alone is one thing. To will the Good, a man must be conscious of himself as an individual, and not just as a face in a crowd. If we will the Good, but only up to a certain point, then we are being double-minded. We must be prepared to accept any kind of suffering or deprivation in our pursuit of the Good. "What kind of life do you live, do you will only one thing, and what is this one thing?" The religious life is based on a leap of faith and we can express our love of God by finding our true vocation in life.

Walden, 1854
Henry David Thoreau

"A man is rich in proportion to the number of things which he can afford to let alone."

WALDEN; OR LIFE IN THE WOODS by Henry David Thoreau is clearly an American classic. It is a much loved book that is often filed in the natural history section of bookstores. But it is also a spiritual classic in its own humble way, as it reflects on the simple life, and the basic virtues that make us human.

The book is about a period of two years, two months, and two days that Thoreau spent living in a cabin near Walden Pond, which is in the woods near to Concord, Massachusetts, on land which was at the time owned by Thoreau's friend Ralph Waldo Emerson. Emerson was known as one of the main figures in the transcendentalist movement.

This was a group of philosophical, literary, and religious ideas that stood in opposition to intellectualism and which stressed man's spiritual and intuitive sides. The transcendentalists were mostly opposed to established religious doctrine, preferring to trust their transcendental intuition.

This was part of the thinking behind Thoreau's experiment with nature. He aimed to live as simply as possible and in a considerable degree of solitude in his cabin. His account of the time he spent there simplifies the actual events in some respects – for instance he compresses the timescale into a year's sojourn.

Thoreau has sometimes been mocked for claiming to live as a hermit whilst staying close to family and friends in Massachusetts, and enjoying meals and social occasions away from his cabin. However he does not pretend otherwise in the actual book, making reference to such occasions and being honest that his seclusion is not the total isolation of a hermit, but a retreat from many of the complexities of modern life.

The book is in many respects a straightforward account of the simple, self-reliant life Thoreau lived. He starts with a chapter on economy where he outlines the four necessities of food, shelter, clothing, and fuel, and examines how simply he could achieve these necessities. He makes it clear that he is not praising poverty as an inherently better condition, merely examining the spiritual benefits that can be achieved by simplifying one's lifestyle. This is one of the messages that will be especially relevant to today's post credit-crunch world.

Thoreau discusses the idea of owning a farm, although he sees the labor involved as more of a millstone than anything. He chooses to live in the cabin, explaining that he wants to "live deliberately, to front only the essential facts of life, and see if I could not learn what it had to teach, and not, when I came to die, discover that I had not lived."

It is in this respect that the spiritual nature of Thoreau's adventure becomes apparent. He is examining his ordinary everyday life by removing as much of it as he possibly can and then, in the absence of clutter and complexity, coming to a clearer understanding of who he is and who he could be.

His life at Walden was far removed from a monastic lifestyle. He extols the virtues of reading classical literature, and entertains a number of interesting visitors, from Emerson himself to a runaway slave. At times his writing on his rural surroundings is quite beautiful, if a touch naïve. He spends one chapter ruminating on all the sounds he can hear in the woods – the noise of the wind in the trees and the wildlife around him, the whip-poor-wills in the trees and the nearby church bell – and contrasting this with the industrial sound of a passing train whistle.

However, he shouldn't be taken to be arguing that we should all live in such rural simplicity at all times. In fact he goes out his way to assert that if anything we need to consider the balance in our lives, between simplicity and sophistication, rather than rejecting all sophistication on principle.

In spite of Thoreau's love of solitude, he is also pleased to receive occasional visitors to his cabin, commenting that if one sits still long enough all kinds of interesting things will come to one's front door.

At one point he takes refuge from a storm in the hut of John Field, a poor laborer who nonetheless holds to the American dream of working hard to achieve a life of luxury. Thoreau fails to persuade him of the benefits of giving up on this dream in favor of a simple life, although Thoreau's comfortable family background makes this story a slightly uncomfortable one for a modern reader.

His life in the book becomes rather more complicated when he is arrested for non-payment of taxes. Thoreau wasn't an anarchist as such, but he was opposed to excessive government and refused to pay taxes to a government that supported slavery. Given his meager earnings from the year (he made about $8 or $9 from the beanfield that he lovingly tended), the amount concerned can't have been too huge, and in fact his aunt paid off the debt after he had spent a single night in jail.

The net effect of these misadventures is a slightly comical one, but Thoreau's writing on non-cooperation has been hugely influential. Gandhi was one famous figure who was inspired by Thoreau's writing on civil disobedience – indeed he borrowed that phrase directly from *Walden* for his own political purposes. Meanwhile Martin Luther King read *Walden* as a young man. He wrote that after reading it, he "became convinced that non-cooperation with evil is as much a moral obligation as is cooperation with good. No other person has been more eloquent and passionate in getting this idea across than Henry David Thoreau."

Toward the end of the book, Thoreau, having survived a winter in his cabin, observes the first growth of spring, as the ice on

Walden Pond melts. This is a moment of epiphany in which one feels that the author is reborn, drawing on all the experiences great and small that he has had in his retreat from the ordinary world.

For many readers, one of the great virtues of *Walden* is the way in which it makes one reflect upon one's own life. You don't need to agree with everything that Thoreau says or thinks to find the idea of his retreat inspiring. And in a world where the materialism and consumerism that Thoreau was reacting against is even more entrenched in everyday culture, the vision he presents of a simple life is a deeply inspiring one to many who sometimes feel overwhelmed by the modern world.

Walden is not a simple rejection of material comforts – instead it is a plea for us to think about each part of our world and to compare it with simpler alternatives. In some respects, such as his love of classical literature, Thoreau believed in a more advanced society than the one in which he lived. In others, such as the degree to which the industrial age has made us into consumers, he raised valid doubts about the direction in which society was headed.

By focusing on self-reliance, close contact with nature and solitude, Thoreau questions the "desperate" existence that he saw as being the life choice of many people, and forces us to consider the ways in which we might be able to improve our own lives by turning away from material things to a more spiritual existence.

Walden

The Speed Read

I withdrew to the solitude of nature in my cabin near Walden Pond for two years, two months, and two days. There I lived a simple life, tending my beans, listening to the sounds of nature in the woods, and only receiving occasional visitors. I spent a night in jail for refusing to pay my taxes to a government that supported slavery, visited friends in town, then returned to the silence of the woods. In the end, my life of self-reliance and simplicity taught me a great deal about who I am.

Leaves from the Notebook
of a Tamed Cynic, 1930
Karl Paul Reinhold Niebuhr

"Without an adequate sermon no clue is given to the moral purpose at the heart of the mystery, and reverence remains without ethical content."

REINHOLD NIEBUHR (1892–1971) was a Protestant theologian who was well known for his work relating theology to the realities of modern life. There are two ways to approach the task of describing his work. One is to take a look at the full sweep of his life and the theological influence he had on his contemporaries and those who came after him. The second is to look at the snapshot of his life as a preacher which is presented by the little book *Leaves from the Notebook of a Tamed Cynic*. This is an account of his time as a young man in Detroit, where he struggles with the responsibilities of a congregation.

Leaves from the Notebook of a Tamed Cynic is not especially representative of Niebuhr's lifetime of writing – he wrote more complex theological works in later life. But it is still his best known work, and an unusually honest and compelling account of the difficulties that face a preacher. He would later refer to this book as an immature work, so it is probably fairest to start with an overview of his life.

He was born in Missouri, studied in Illinois, Missouri, and Yale, before being ordained a pastor in the German Evangelical church in 1915. He was sent to serve in Detroit, where his congregation numbered less than 100 people. This was a time of great industrial growth in the town and by 1928 when he moved on, his church had grown to 700 members.

At this stage Niebuhr was a pacifist. He also became involved in social causes, campaigning against the industrial practices of the manufacturer and against the Klu Klux Klan in particular. In 1928, he published *Leaves from the Notebook of a Tamed Cynic*, a journal of his time in Detroit. From there he moved on the New York City, where he became a Professor of Practical Theology at Union Theological Seminary. His lectures there were highly influential on a generation of students, including Dietrich Bonhoeffer who traveled from Germany to New York in the 1930s.

The Second World War proved a significant challenge to Niebuhr's pacifism and communist sympathies. He gradually came to believe in the idea of a just war and to support the military fight against fascism and communism. This was a dark, challenging time for the world, and Niebuhr was forced to face up to the idea that one might have to choose the lesser of two evils when faced with tyranny.

His 1952 book *The Irony of American History* captures the transformation of his views to the "Christian Realism" he now espoused. His thinking of this period is also presented in *The Nature and Destiny of Man,* a collection of the Gifford Lectures, which he gave in Edinburgh in the 1940s. He retained some of his former beliefs and always campaigned for social justice, but this was now grounded in a different framework of beliefs about the world and the necessity for democracy to defend its freedom. He saw the United States as a nation in which hard won freedoms could be used as a basis to move toward a society of greater social equality and justice.

His thinking was influential on Martin Luther King, among others, in particular the vision of the United States as a mythological agent of justice, and of a future in which the United States' freedoms would create a better land for all. Fifty years later, we also find Barack Obama quoting Niebuhr's influence:

I take away . . . the compelling idea that there's serious evil in the world, and hardship and pain. And we should be humble and modest in our belief we can eliminate those things. But we shouldn't use that as an excuse for cynicism and inaction. I take away . . . the sense we have to make these efforts knowing they are hard, and not swinging from naïve idealism to bitter realism.

Niebuhr's influence has in other respects waned as his Christian realism was superseded by other movements within Protestant theology. But he is still a writer that theologians take seriously, and in whose writing there is much of value.

Going back to *Leaves from the Notebook of a Tamed Cynic*, one can see why Niebuhr saw the book as a piece of writing from a far earlier, more innocent period of his life. However, while the book contains little of the complexities of his later theology, it is a wonderful read in a very different way.

By writing so engagingly about the problems he faced in Detroit, Niebuhr gives a very clear picture of life as a preacher. He talks of the difficulties he has in thinking of new subjects for sermons, the inspiration he takes from his parishioners, and the fact that he sometimes feels intimidated by them. He discusses the fact that there can be more spirituality in a factory or a front room than in a church where the sermon is uninspired. At one point he writes that:

A prophet speaks only when he is inspired. The parish preacher must speak whether he is inspired or not. I wonder whether it is possible to live on a high enough plane to do that without sinning against the Holy Spirit.

And in writing of these problems he also brings out the fact that ministry is a two way process. The pastor may leave the seminary full of confidence and belief in the grace of God, but he comes up against the realities of people's lives and learns as much from them as they do from him. We see him progress through the war years and on to a more mature understanding of his place, and at every step of the process there are illuminations from his intelligence and humility in the face of the challenges he faces.

Spirituality can be a private experience, one in which we withdraw from the world or go into retreat to examine our own minds and our relationship with God. But far more often, our spiritual lives are part of our life in the community we inhabit. In our daily struggles, worries, and joys, we find our own path, and we learn from the paths of those around us.

Niebuhr's book is well known as an introductory text for young preachers who can learn from his experiences. But it has something to say to anyone who sees their spirituality in the context of their community and who thinks they can either teach or learn from others as part of everyday life.

Leaves from the Notebook of a Tamed Cynic

The Speed Read

"There is something ludicrous about a callow young fool like myself standing up to preach a sermon to these good folks. I talk wisely about life and know little about life's problems." In my time as a pastor in Detroit, I learn as much from those good folks as they do from me. And one thing I come to understand is that I must always stay humble in the face of these problems, but that a good sermon can be the difference between a spiritual moment and a church that feels empty.

Gravity and Grace, 1947
Simone Weil

*"It is only the impossible that is possible for God.
He has given over the possible to the mechanics of matter
and the autonomy of his creatures."*

S IMONE WEIL IS A fascinating figure in the history of spiritual writing. She was a French philosopher and social activist who was born in Paris in 1909. In her early life she was drawn to the radical politics of Marxism and anarchism that was prevalent in the period. She campaigned on behalf of the proletariat and the poor, and tried to fight in the Spanish Civil War, although her chronic ill health defeated her in this ambition.

She was a contemporary of Simone de Beauvoir's at the Ecole Normal Superieure and became a teacher of philosophy. Most of the writing for which she is remembered was published posthumously. This includes some interesting philosophical and political thought, but the aspect of her thinking which is of interest here is best represented by the book *Gravity and Grace.*

This is an aphoristic collection which was compiled by Gustav Thibon, and was made up of selections from her notebooks. Weil had experienced a religious epiphany in 1937 while in a church in Assisi, in the same place where St Francis had once prayed. From this time onward her writing and thinking started to take a more spiritual angle, even when she was dealing with social issues. Thibon was a devout Catholic – Weil herself decided not to be baptized into the church (she was from a Jewish family), although she did study under a Dominican friar.

However, while Weil was against any attempt to synthesize religions and reduce them a universal religion, she believed that there were many different paths to God. She was also fascinated by other religious sources such as the Upanishads and Mahayana Buddhism. And even within Christian tradition, she took her own path, being influenced by works as varied as those of the Philokalia and St John of the Cross.

She also focused strongly on the New Testament, largely rejecting the role of the Old Testament in her view of the world. We need to remember while reading *Gravity and Grace* that this is a selection that has been made by a friend with a particular interpretation of her work. However Thibon does not intrude his own interpretations of her work. Instead we are left to comprehend her subtle thinking for ourselves.

One part of her writing focused on the problem of evil, and how we can reconcile this with God's love. She views the world as being caused by God's love, but also she stresses the importance of the idea of absence in this. God's perfection means that our creation and existence is something that happens to some degree in the absence of God. The afflictions and evil that we feel are not punishments or injustices but something that propels us in the direction of God. In other words the only way we could come into existence at all as imperfect beings was to be less than holy.

When Weil talks about affliction she speaks of something more than mere suffering. She suffered from very poor health herself. She was also prone to bringing suffering on herself in sympathy with those for whom she campaigned. Even at the age of six she was refusing to eat sugar in sympathy with the soldiers at the Western Front.

Later in life she was driven to try to live life like the poor and unemployed for whom she felt a strong empathy. Even her early death in 1943 was partly caused by this tendency – following a period of illness in exile in England, she refused to eat as well as she could have done to recover, preferring to restrict her eating to the rations that she felt that her compatriots in occupied France were being kept to. Sadly, this contributed to her death.

These anecdotes reveal someone who showed a level of sensitivity to the suffering of others that could even be characterized as neurotic, and that certainly led to self-destructive behaviors. But they can also be seen as saintly, or at least spiritual impulses. Affliction for Weil was something that affected those souls who were closest to spiritual growth – the realization of suffering was therefore part of the path toward God's love.

One must also remember that Weil lived in a period of great suffering. Her childhood was in the shadow of the First World War, she then lived through the deprivations of the Depression, before going into the Second World War in which her country was once again invaded. In her short life there was little peace and much suffering and she was driven to try to understand the reasons for this in her writing.

So in her analysis of suffering, Weil was both urging us to try to see the world from the point of view of the oppressed, poor, and miserable (a message that echoes the sayings of Jesus) and also arguing that affliction was in itself a spiritual opening. She described affliction as being like God holding one's hand tightly, pressing hard, and said that if we could get beyond the sound of our own lamentations, we would discover the silence of God beneath.

The separation we feel from God is for Weil something that is partly illusory. She uses an old term from Greek philosophy, *metaxu,* which means something that both connects and separates at the same time. She uses the metaphor of a blind man's stick to describe the way that the physical world both separates us from God, but at the same time allows us a way to feel and grope our way toward him. His very absence in the physical world is something which we can use to start thinking about his reality.

Beyond *Gravity and Grace,* Weil's spirituality also shines through in her political writing. She interprets the golden rule of Jesus in terms of obligations, and the obligation we have to respect and love others. She also speaks of spirituality as a very everyday part of our lives.

For her the religious practices of icons such as St Francis or St

John of the Cross give us lessons in how we can start to approach the affliction of our lives, and also in how we must empathize with those more wretched than ourselves. Thus politics and spirituality become intertwined in her thinking.

Gravity and Grace is a curious book to read. It doesn't present a consistent, ordered argument, as it is a series of selections from notebooks. The first thing that strikes one is that much of the writing is beautiful and inspiring, but it takes a while to discern a wider picture of Weil's spiritual beliefs. But this is a book that repays patience and that has become a beloved favorite of many readers over time.

Gravity and Grace

The Speed Read

Simone Weil's aphoristic collection, in which suffering is seen as a path to Godliness. In her view, the problem of evil arises from the fact that we must be born as imperfect beings, and the afflictions of life thus lead us in the direction of God and his love.

One Day in the Life of
Ivan Denisovich, 1962
Aleksandr Solzenhitzyn

"You should rejoice that you're in prison.
Here you have time to think about your soul."

ONE DAY IN THE LIFE OF IVAN DENISOVICH is an interesting book for a number of reasons. Historically, it is the legacy of a very particular period of Russian history. The author Aleksandr Solzenhitzyn had been a victim of Stalin's repression. Having been a loyal Soviet citizen and soldier, he wrote a letter toward the end of the Second World War questioning the tactics of the leaders and referring to Stalin derogatorily as "the whiskered one."

For this "crime" he ended up spending eight years in the labor camps in the Gulag. He was not released until 1953, having spent many years in the harsh environment of the camps. Between 1957 and 1962 he worked on a book that was a lightly fictionalized account of his time in prison. At the time this was more or less unpublishable due to the censorship in the Soviet regime.

However the intellectual atmosphere thawed somewhat when Khrushchev came to power. Solzenhitzyn approached the editor of *Novy Mir*, a literary magazine, and he was deeply impressed by the book. He submitted the book to the Soviet Central Committee for permission to publish it and it was eventually sanctioned by Khrushchev himself, albeit with a few minor revisions.

The publication of *One Day in the Life of Ivan Denisovich*, initially in *Novy Mir*, was a sensation in Russian life. Many had not known much of the Gulag, and those who knew that it existed did not know the level of detail that was exposed in the book. The vagaries of Soviet life meant that since the regime now embraced Solzenhitzyn, he became for a few years a celebrity who was fully supported by the regime.

However as the mood of liberalisation faded, once Khrushchev was ousted from power, Solzenhitzyn ended up being censored and repressed again. He ended up as a non-person, and was eventually deported, not returning to his beloved Russia until many years later in the post-communist period of glasnost.

Meanwhile, Solzenhitzyn's international reputation had been made by his powerful writing in *One Day in the Life of Ivan Denisovich*. The book centers on Ivan Denisovich Shukhov, who has been imprisoned in the camps after being falsely accused of being a spy. The book is fictionalized, but is clearly based closely on Solzenhitzyn's own time in the camps.

The spiritual aspects of the book come from the way that it deals with human nature and the way that we react to hardship. There are different types of people in the camps. Some of the warders represent genuine sadism and evil, while others are simply doing their job while failing to acknowledge the immorality of the situation.

Meanwhile the lives of the prisoners revolve around tiny triumphs and setbacks. The acquisition of food or a few moments of snatched warmth in the miserable, freezing Siberian cold become of overwhelming importance. Shukhov spends time queuing to get supplies that he can swap for favours. The prisoners sometimes help each other, but always with a knowledge that there is a limit to how far they can go. But the strength of their spirits shines through in the tiny details of the terrible life that they are enduring.

In Ivan Denisovich, we see the way that a man can lower his expectations to deal with a terrible life. The small achievements of his day come to him as moments of great joy. He delights in seeing the sun at its height, meaning that it is nearly lunchtime and the morning of hard graft has passed faster than it might have done.

Rather than focusing on the setbacks he encounters throughout the day, or the terrible nature of his plight, he ends up seeing the day as a good one – at the end of the day he "went to sleep fully content. He'd had many strokes of luck that day."

Denisovich also focuses on the way that a prisoner maximizes the pleasure he gets from his few free moments – first thing in the morning, last thing at night, and in the brief meal breaks. At these times, he can be still within himself, for a few moments free of the constant supervision, roll calls, searches, and fear of punishment.

The book can even be enjoyable to read as it focuses on the more positive side of this equation, but it leaves the reader in absolutely no doubt as to how dehumanizing the camps are – the very things that Denisovich escapes from in these moments are a terrible source of anxiety and worry that rob the prisoners of much of their dignity, leaving them having to scrabble after small favors.

This is a brilliant book, one that illuminates a terrible time in history and the spiritual costs of imprisonment in a deep but simple way. As a study in humanity in times of hardship and injustice, it is hard to better. We see both the terrible injustice of the overall situation, and the small ways in which the human spirit can still triumph.

As we gradually realize that this is a good day for Ivan Denisovich because of the small things that go right, we simultaneously know that the bad days must be truly terrible ones. And we know that tens of thousands of people suffered this fate under Stalin, many never winning their release, just as many people today continue to suffer imprisonment on unjust grounds.

It can also be a book that gives us spiritual consolation in very different situations. No matter how bad our lives may seem, few of us suffer deprivations of hardships as bad as the figures in the Stalinist labor camps. Ivan Denisovich's ability to find joy in small moments through his day is an inspiration to remember that if we live in the here and now, there are many things we should give thanks for. This book can be a reminder that difficulties can be transcended if only we can find the right way to make our life into a spiritual celebration.

One Day in the Life of Ivan Denisovich

The Speed Read

Ivan Denisovich is woken at five a.m. in the freezing cold by a hammer banging on the rail of his prison hut. He is serving ten years in the Gulag for false accusations of crimes against the state. For waking late, since he is sick, he is forced to clean the guardhouse. He spends the day in hard labour with the 104 squad, conserving any food he can, and treasuring the small moments he gets of peace and solitude. In the evening he trades services with fellow inmate Tsezar in return for scraps of extra food. He goes to bed content. It has been one of the good days.

Poustinia, 1975
Catherine Doherty

*"Acquire inner peace and a multitude will find
their salvation near you."*

C ATHERINE DOHERTY was born and baptized as a Russian
Orthodox Christian. After she emigrated to the United
States and Canada, she popularized the Orthodox idea of
poustinia in the West. A poustinia is a small cabin, furnished in the
most minimal way possible, to which one retreats to pray and fast.
The literal translation of poustinia is "desert" and this gives a sense
of the condition of isolation that one might expect from such a
retreat. In this condition of solitude, one can feel that one is in the
presence of God.

In Russia there was a strong tradition of hermits and starets
(religious leaders) living in poustinia, and in some cases staying
there permanently (in which case they were known as *poustiniks.*

Catherine Doherty's own life made a fascinating story. She
helped to set up retreats and poustinias in North America, and
had many disagreements with the established church. In
particular she fought for economic justice and against racial
segregation when these were not mainstream church policies. She
also worked extensively with the poor, sometimes living in poverty
herself.

In Ontario, she set up Madonna House, a Catholic lay community offering a retreat from the "marketplace" of the ordinary
world. The houses there were communal quarters, in which those
who went on retreat renounced individual ownership. At

Madonna House one could choose a life of spiritual modesty, and embrace old-fashioned vows of chastity, obedience, and poverty. The established church gradually embraced her slightly maverick approach and the retreat movement is now a far stronger part of the Catholic Church in particular.

It was against this background that she wrote her widely regarded book *Poustinia*. The book champions the ideal of the poustinia as a spiritual remedy. In essence the purpose of a poustinia is to use the solitude to search for meaning. One eats only bread and water, for anything from four to 30 days. The only reading material provided is the Bible. One might take short walks, or exercise. One might choose to sleep long hours. One might pray if inspiration leads that way, but it is not the only way in which such a retreat can provide spiritual consolation. Catherine Doherty had overseen many people who went through this process at Madonna House and as a result had a deep under-standing of the process and of its merits.

She believed that in the confusion of the modern world, the search for silence was even more important that ever before:

> *It seems strange to say, but what can help modern man find the answers to his own mystery and the mystery of him in whose image he is created, is silence, solitude – in a word, the desert. Modern man needs these things more than the hermits of old.*

Doherty also relates her Western retreat to memories of her Russian childhood and the hermits and starets that she encoun-tered. She describes Peter, a friend of her father, who gave up his wealth to wander alone, a barefoot pilgrim (reminiscent of the narrator of *The Way of the Pilgrim,* or the original Franciscans who heeded Christ's exhortation to travel barefoot and in poverty).

Years later her father spotted this friend, apparently an idiot, among a group of beggars. When he spoke to him, his old self returned to his face and he embraced his old friend. When her father asked him why he was abasing himself in this way, he replied that he was atoning for all those men who had called Christ a fool during his life and in the many centuries since.

Such memories, and those of the hermits who would live on the edge of town in a self-imposed solitude, tolerating visitors but not inviting them, obviously made a deep impression on Doherty. She goes on to describe the set-up of Madonna House, and the conditions under which those undergoing a poustinia would live. The book also includes talks and addresses given to staff and visitors to the community.

This is an inspiring book in two separate ways. Firstly the whole idea of setting up such a community and of bringing the Russian tradition of hermits and solitude into Western religion is an intriguing one and something that has been a valuable experiment. But secondly, the idea of a retreat from the modern world is one that seems increasingly rare and hard to achieve.

Whether we find our own way of fulfilling Doherty's idea of how a poustinia should operate, or whether we seek to make a formal retreat from life, there can be great value from taking an ascetic break and re-evaluating our life and direction. Whether it is a religious experience or a simple break from life it is something that clearly has a great appeal to the modern mindset. Sadly it is one that only seems to be achieved for some people in rehabiliation, rather than in the purer surroundings of a poustinia.

One can understand why this simple book has been such an enduring spiritual classic and why so many people have been inspired by it to take a long look at their own lives and to wonder whether a period of genuine silence and solitude may be the remedy their soul is waiting for.

Poustinia

The Speed Read

In my childhood I was familiar with the Russian Orthodox tradition of poustinia. This is a retreat where one lives in solitude and silence and through prayer and reflection comes into the presence of God. It is something we need more than ever in the modern world, The modern person who undergoes a poustinia can take the solitude of the desert back into their everyday life with them, and live a better life rooted in this experience.

Lives of Inspiration

Lives of Inspiration: Introduction

O NE OF THE MOST inspiring things about reading spiritual classics is the way that it exposes us to the stories of people who have lived remarkable lives. In this section we have gathered some of the books which focus on individuals who, for one reason or another, can be seen as an example or inspiration to us in our own lives.

The first two selections are the journals of two well known figures from the Quaker movement: George Fox and John Woolman. Each in their own way showed great bravery and persistence in the face of adversity. Fox was largely responsible for founding the Society of Friends, but his message of listening to one's inner light was unwelcome to those of more orthodox views and he had to be a man of extraordinary talents to overcome the opposition he faced. Whereas John Woolman's opposition to slavery was one of the turning points in American attitudes to that iniquitous institution, and a brave stance for him to take against the contemporary flow of ideas.

Leo Tolstoy is interesting for different reasons. Here is someone who had drifted away from religion, but was brave enough to rethink all his assumptions in life. He re-examined the foundations of Christian belief and realized that his earlier rejection of spirituality had been for weak reasons. He also had to persist in the face of a different kind of opposition, which was that his new thinking was unpopular within his own family, something that caused him a good deal of unhappiness. Thomas Merton (*The Seven-Storey Mountain*) may not have suffered in the same way, but he made a similarly brave decision to reassess his life and to make a commitment to the religious life.

In Dietrich Bonhoeffer (*The Cost of Discipleship*) and Watchman Nee (*The Normal Christian Life*) we see two writers who went through extremes of suffering for their beliefs. In the early church many Christians showed great bravery in being martyred for their beliefs. Bonhoeffer's bravery in standing up to the Nazis shows a similar degree of courage, and we are lucky to have his own account of how he views the problem of conscience and discipleship to Jesus. Meanwhile, Watchman Nee also made the decision to stay in his own country in spite of a repressive regime. In his case he suffered from 20 years of imprisonment for his beliefs.

The remaining books in this section each deal with lives that are inspirational in one way or another. Mother Theresa and Jean Vanier both showed considerable self-sacrifice and love in their charity and generosity toward those less fortunate than themselves.

Of course there are many other writers and books that could have been included in this section. The final selections are each books that have a certain beauty and wisdom, but there have been many people throughout history who have lived good lives that should continue to inspire us today.

The Journal of George Fox, 1694
George Fox

"Then the Lord let me see why there was none upon the earth that could speak to my condition, namely, that I might give Him all the glory; for all are concluded under sin, and shut up in unbelief as I had been, that Jesus Christ might have the pre-eminence who enlightens, and gives grace, and faith, and power."

GEORGE FOX (1624–1691) was the principal founder of the Religious Society of Friends, usually known as the Quakers. He lived through a tumultuous period of history, which included both the English Civil War and the restoration of the monarchy. This was time of fervent discussion of political and theological thinking, with groups such as the Ranters, Levellers and Diggers being well known as radical exponents of new thinking.

Fox was a rather eccentric figure, who liked to rebel against authority. His parents had hoped he might become a priest but he was not impressed by the conventions of the established church. He became a traveling preacher in 1647 after experiencing a series of visions.

(There has been some interesting debate about Fox's mental state of mind – he suffered from severe depressions and mood swings – and whether or not one should take this into account when judging his teachings.)

In his preaching Fox rejected any part of the church that he could not regard as being based on the bible. In this respect he was a part of the mainstream Protestant religion that had developed over the centuries since ordinary people had gained access to scripture and had been able to make their own judgments as to whether the Church was based on the teachings of Jesus or not.

Fox was also opposed to the idea that worship needed a church, derisively calling them "steeple-houses" and arguing that one could worship God anywhere, and that anyone could lead prayer, even women and children (a view that was deeply controversial at the time). He encouraged his followers to trust their "inner light" and to have a direct relationship with God. The Quakers refused to take oaths, they were against slavery and war, and they emphasized personal, spiritual experience over formal religious practice.

Predictably, the Quakers (including Fox) were widely attacked for their beliefs both in Fox's native England and in other countries in Europe. Fox was imprisoned on eight separate occasions. He argued passionately for tolerance of his beliefs and managed in turn to persuade both Oliver Cromwell and Charles II to lessen their persecution.

He was a passionate exponent of his beliefs, and rather fond of arguing. He would often go to church services and start debates with the priests on theological grounds. As an example of his argumentative nature, his court appearances were marked by arguments with the judges as to whether the Bible insisted that defendants should wear hats or not. He was also frequently attacked or beaten as he traveled around preaching, by those who took exception to his beliefs.

He traveled widely in Europe and the United States and inspired a wide variety of responses, from those who considered him dangerous or mad to those who came under his influence. The Quaker movement grew after his death into the worldwide institution that it is today, and while later Quakers moved away from Fox's position on some issues, his basic beliefs lie at the heart of Quakerism.

The Journal of George Fox was first published in 1694. It was edited by Thomas Ellwood, a friend of John Milton's and had a preface by William Penn, who had traveled with Fox, and had founded the American Quaker colony of Pennsylvania. The Journal was partly dictated by Fox, although parts were constructed by the editors and written as though they were his work.

It is the story of Fox's life, his visions, imprisonments, and travels. It is a dense read, probably best first read in a shorter abridgement. But it contains a great deal of fascinating writing, and gives us a clear picture of the times Fox lived in, and of the awkward, questioning, loving figure that he was. One can see why he inspired such respect. Walt Whitman, whose parents were inspired by Quaker thought, wrote that: "George Fox stands for something too – a thought – the thought that wakes in silent hours – perhaps the deepest, most eternal thought latent in the human soul. This is the thought of God, merged in the thoughts of moral right and the immortality of identity. Great, great is this thought – aye, greater than all else."

Quakers were often accused of antinomianism, which means that they were thought to be saying that they were beyond the existing religious law and subject only to their own consciences. The history of the Christian churches is an ongoing struggle between those who asserted various orthodoxies and those who sought to challenge or rebel against them.

Fox's journal presents us with a fascinating case study in the virtues of rejecting orthodoxy. From a modern viewpoint, a great deal of what he believed in seems self-evident. He was in favor of a simpler church in which all were together in brotherhood or sisterhood. He was rebelling against the dominance of ceremony, established tradition and rote learning in favor of a more passionate, personal spirituality. That, in making this points, he had to struggle against persecution and wilful incomprehension makes him an inspiring figure to us today.

The Journal of George Fox

The Speed Read

We have an inner light that connects us to Jesus. True religion doesn't come from obedience to ritual but from personal spiritual conversion. It is the Holy Spirit that qualifies one to be a minister, not theological study. God is within us all and we can feel his presence. We can worship him anywhere as he is present in all places, not just in the "steeple-house" of established religion. I have traveled England and the world teaching these lessons, in spite of many imprisonments and beatings along the way.

The Journal of John Woolman, 1772
John Woolman

*"As I looked to the Lord, he inclined my heart to His testimony.
I told the man that I believed the practice of continuing slavery
to this people was not right."*

O FTEN THE MOST inspiring books to read are those that recount the simple facts about a spiritual life. John Woolman's *Journal* is one such book. Woolman was a Quaker preacher, who traveled around the American colonies in the eighteenth century. He was an opponent of slavery, and always an advocate of peace and understanding rather than military and domestic force and violence. The book is Woolman's own account of his life and beliefs.

He was born in 1720, into a family of Friends (Quakers), who had been among the earliest settlers of New Jersey. One of the earliest recollections he gives in the *Journal* is of an incident that happened when he was a young boy. He found a robin's nest with young robins inside. Being a foolish young boy, he started throwing rocks at the mother robin, and ended up killing her. He realized that the baby robins would not survive without her, so for the sake of mercy took the nest down and killed them too.

While many young people might shrug or laugh this off, the young Woolman pondered what he had done and became full of remorse. He would always remember this feeling in later life – he wrote:

In this case I believed that Scripture proverb was fulfilled, "The tender mercies of the wicked are cruel." I then went on my errand,

and for some hours could think of little else but the cruelties I had committed, and was much troubled. Thus He whose tender mercies are over all His works hath placed a principle in the human mind, which incites to exercise goodness towards every living creature; and this being singly attended to, people become tender-hearted and sympathizing; but when frequently and totally rejected, the mind becomes shut up in a contrary disposition.

So from an early age Woolman developed a sense of love and protectiveness for all living creatures. This would also influence his thinking in a different way when he was older, following another incident that became a turning point. When he was 23 years old he was asked to write a bill of sale for a slave. He did so out of duty to his employer, but writes that: "at the executing of it I was so afflicted in my mind, that I said before my master and the Friend that I believed slave-keeping to be a practice inconsistent with the Christian religion."

This was a time when the Friends had not settled on a consistent theory with regard to the practice of slavery. Many individuals may have been uneasy with the widespread keeping of slaves in the new colonies and regarded it as a sin, but like Woolman, they suppressed their doubts or withheld from a universal condemnation of the practice. However Woolman, rather than try to shake off his unease, carried his concerns through into action. He started to personally campaign against slavery.

From this time onward he traveled widely through the colonies. He was non-confrontational in his approach, but persuaded many individual Quakers that slavery was wrong. Some of those Friends had acquired slaves in order to treat them better than their original owners, but now Woolman argued that the relationship of master and slave between two human beings was innately wrong. Her refused to use goods such as dyed clothes or silver cups and plates that he believed to have been produced using slave labor. He also insisted on paying other people's slaves for any labor they did from which he benefitted.

Woolman was even sensitive to the use of animals for forced labor, often preferring to avoid the use of stagecoaches where he felt the horses were being treated unkindly. A large part of Woolman's argument was about the inequality between people. He was against slavery in all cases, but was more forgiving of those slave-owners who worked in tandem with their slaves and treated them well than he was of those who lived a life of ease on the back of their slaves' labors.

No one man could defeat such a widespread practice as slavery single-handed. But what Woolman did achieve was to bring about significant changes in attitudes. His book *Some Considerations on the Keeping of Negroes* was published in 1754 and widely read, while his *Journal*, published in 1772, remained in print for centuries to come. During his lifetime, a large part of the Quaker movement traveled from uncertainty about slavery to a more robust condemnation of the practice, and this was very influential in the increasing campaign to have slavery abolished over coming years.

Woolman also campaigned on other issues – in the spirit of his belief that humans of all races should be treated with equality, he spoke directly to Native Americans in a time when many disdained them as savages. He also refused to pay taxes when he believed they were going to support contemporary wars. But it is his achievements in helping to turn the tide against slavery for which he is best remembered.

The *Journal* tells the story of his preaching and opposition to slavery with great simplicity. His spirituality is an inspiring example for anyone reading it, which is one reason why the book has been so enduringly popular. It is also a fascinating historical document. Woolman was traveling in the American colonies before the United States became independent. This was a time of great political and moral uncertainty. A nation was being shaped and it was as yet uncertain what shape that nation would take. It is to the great credit of John Woolman that he was able to help guide it toward a future in which slavery was regarded as unacceptable.

The Journal of John Woolman

The Speed Read

As a young man I killed a family of robins. I felt such remorse I vowed to be kind to my fellow creatures in future. At the age of 23 I wrote a bill of sale for a slave, but again my conscience spoke and I knew that it was wrong for any man to keep another as a slave. I traveled the early American colonies spreading the message of peace and campaigning against slavery, and this journal records those travels for posterity.

A Confession, 1884
Leo Tolstoy

"The whole of the people possessed a knowledge of the truth, for otherwise they could not have lived. Moreover, that knowledge was accessible to me, for I had felt it and had lived by it. But I no longer doubted that there was also falsehood in it. … But where did the truth and where did the falsehood come from? Both the falsehood and the truth were contained in the so-called holy tradition and in the Scriptures. Both the falsehood and the truth had been handed down by what is called the Church."

LEO TOLSTOY, OR Count Lev Nikolayevich (1828–1910) was one of the greatest novelists ever. His two best known works, *War and Peace* and *Anna Karenina* are each in their separate ways among the very finest of novels. But Tolstoy was also a remarkable spiritual thinker, especially in his later years.

The turning point in Tolstoy's thought came with the short book *A Confession*, which was first distributed in Russia in 1882 before being published two years later. In his two great novels he had taken a rationalist position – he describes the philosophical message of those books in *A Confession* as being "that one should live so as to have the best for oneself and one's family."

He had also taken the position that history was an inexorable process in which one could have little control over one's life. This led Tolstoy to suggest a rather passive submission to one's place in life. But by the later stages of *Anna Karenina*, Tolstoy had come to find his own philosophical position unsatisfactory and he turned back to religion for solutions.

A Confession is written in the form of autobiographical notes on how Tolstoy's religious beliefs had been formulated and modified over time. In searching for the meaning of life, Tolstoy no longer found a passive acceptance of fate to be an acceptable solution. He had lost his faith in Christianity at a young age. However, looking back, he came to feel that what he had lost faith in was partly the church itself and the mixture of truth and falsehood he saw it as enshrining.

After eliminating such possible solutions as science and eastern wisdom, as well as existing political theory, Tolstoy moves on to acknowledging the simple Christian faith of everyday people as being of the utmost importance. While he feels that there are always falsehoods among those beliefs, he no longer feels that this is a reason to reject faith per se.

Instead he returns to the New Testament to make his own decisions as to what he can still have faith in. This means that he chooses to reject some of the positions and customs of the Christian church as he saw it (meaning the Russian Orthodox church of his time, and other established Christian churches in Europe).

In particular Tolstoy focused on the moral lessons of the Gospels, in particular the Sermon on the Mount. He takes Christ's injunction to "turn the other cheek" with the utmost seriousness and explores its meaning for us today. He concludes from this that the only political means to achieve change must be pacifism, and non-violence.

Tolstoy's political beliefs at this time were somewhat com-munistic or more accurately anarchistic – he rejected the compul-sion of the state and the organization of a central church. However his non-violence led him to reject the communist and anarchist calls for violent revolution. In this way he would come to be a significant influence on twentieth-century figures such as Gandhi and Martin Luther King who also chose passive resistance as their preferred means of struggle against oppression.

Some of the specifics of these ideas were spelled out more clearly in his later books, *My Religion*, *The Kingdom of God is Within You* (which became one of Gandhi's inspirations) and *The Gospels in Brief*. But *A Confession* remains the most powerful statement of Tolstoy's spiritual crisis and journey to the kind of Christian anarchism that marked his later years.

As a result of his religious writings, Tolstoy gathered a following who regarded themselves as Tolstoyans rather than as Orthodox Christians. He became a cult figure and intellectuals and spiritual leaders from across Europe would travel to his home to speak to the great man.

Ironically it is this very celebrity that gives one most pause for thought in reassessing Tolstoy's spiritual significance today. Even in *A Confession* there is a tendency to self-aggrandisement, of a very subtle kind, but that makes one feel that Tolstoy is not merely putting forward spiritual ideas but also asserting his own importance. In his fame he came almost to be seen as the founder of a new religion and, while his later years were not his happiest (because his family was estranged by his new beliefs), this perhaps affected his writing on spiritual matters adversely. While reading, one tends to wonder if the importance of his writing was overrated by contemporaries, who were judging his importance partly on the basis of his astonishing literary work.

However in its most simple and humble moments, *A Confession* is still a powerful book. It is an account of a serious and deep thinker who wants to understand why their faith has been allowed to lapse and who chooses to contemplate Christ's actual words to try to rediscover that faith. We may not share all of Tolstoy's conclusions, especially those which are too closely related to the political theories of their time, but we can admire the sincerity of his exploration of the meaning of life.

A Confession

The Speed Read

When I was very young I accepted religion, but as I grew older I lost my faith as I rejected the weary ritual and formalities of the church. As I grew older and sought the meaning of life I came to find all other explanations unsatisfying, so I returned to Christ's words to examine the real meaning, especially his Sermon on the Mount. As a result I came to realize that the simple faith of everyday folks should not be rejected merely because it contains some falsehoods. Instead we should focus on the part of that simple faith that we can recognize to be the truth.

The Cost of Discipleship, 1937
Dietrich Bonhoeffer

"Cheap grace is the mortal enemy of our church.
Our struggle today is for costly grace."

ONE OF THE MOST uncomfortable questions one can ask oneself about history is to ponder how you might have reacted to the rise of Hitler if you had been able to oppose the rise of Nazism. Which of us can be absolutely sure that we would have the moral strength to resist a dictatorship, even to our own cost?

The life of Dietrich Bonhoeffer provides one inspiring example of someone who refused to be cowed by the Nazis and refused to accept that his church would not stand up to them. *The Cost of Discipleship* is his most widely read book, and makes a strong argument about how the church and the individual should react to the modern world, in the context of a brutal, repressive government. The book centers on Bonhoeffer's extended meditations on the Sermon on the Mount and his thoughts on what Jesus was asking of his followers.

Bonhoeffer was born in 1906. He became a theologian and Lutheran pastor and traveled widely, including a visit to New York, as part of his studies. He returned to Germany in 1931, and would become a founding member of the Confessing Church, a branch of the church which opposed the Nazis' ideology and actions. He was friends with the theologian Karl Barth and their conversations in the 1930s centered on the liberal theology of the Lutheran church.

Bonhoeffer came to feel that the emphasis on personal experience and engagement with society was in some respects being used to elevate human society over the teaching of Christ in the scriptures. Together with Barth he was known as a neo-orthodox thinker, meaning that they believed that it was important to go back to the word of God as revealed in the Bible, rather than trusting to the complex orthhodoxies that had built up over the eighteenth and nineteenth centuries within the Protestant tradition.

Bonhoeffer lived in Britain in the mid-1930s, but returned to Germany at a time when his Confessing Church was being suppressed by the SS. He did this even though, in a 1933 radio address, he had denounced Hitler and also denounced the German people for allowing themselves to be led by a corrupt, evil leader and regime, describing Hitler as a false idol. This obviously put him in immediate danger within Germany.

In spite of the bans imposed upon his church he continued to lead it in its opposition to the anti-semitic Nazi drive. The Confessing Church was a reproach to both the official German church and the Roman Catholic hierarchies, which failed to engage with or oppose Hitler in any meaningful way.

Bonhoeffer was banned from preaching, from teaching, and finally from any kind of public speaking whatsoever by the regime. He became involved with opponents of the Nazis and played some part in a plot to assassinate Hitler. He was finally arrested after money that had been used by Jews escaping to Switzerland across the border was traced back to him.

Once the plot to assassinate Hitler failed in 1944, his connections to the conspirators were revealed, and his fate was sealed. He was moved around a succession of prisons and concentration camps before being executed in a brutal hanging at Flossenburg in April 1945. The end of the war was only a matter of weeks away, but he would not live to send the destruction of the regime he had done so much to oppose.

His writings survived as a record of his beliefs and life. *The Cost of Discipleship* was written in 1937 and takes a look at the meaning of following Jesus. He points out that Jesus' call is for us to "come and die." He is asking us to give up our entire lives for him, not to do things by halves. He is not necessarily asking us to die as martyrs, but to consider our relationship with Christ deeply, to be sure that we know that we are doing all that we possibly can do to follow him.

He contrasts "cheap grace" and "costly grace." The former is the kind of grace that one bestows on oneself when one imagines one is living a holy life, without truly examining that life or engaging with Christ. The latter is a far more committed form of grace in which we truly ask ourselves if we are living up to the demands that Christ placed upon us as believers.

For Bonhoeffer, it is not enough to turn up to Church on a Sunday and bask in the glory of praying in front of the community. He sees public prayer as a matter of display and argues that only our private prayer and engagement will allow us to communicate with God.

Bonhoeffer's prose is at times offputting. He can be a harsh writer, especially as he is so insistent on sacrifice, and his theological detail can be intimidating. But his core message is a powerful one. He argues that too many Christians want to know exactly where the path to God will lead them, but instead urges readers to "plunge into the deep waters beyond your own comprehension, and I will help you to comprehend even as I do."

One also has to place Bonhoeffer's insistence on the pain, suffering, and sacrifice we will experience, as part of our discipleship, in the context of the dark times in which he was writing. For him, following his conscience was an intensely dangerous path. He could have stayed away from Germany and preached against Hitler from a distance, but his conscience drove him to re-enter the country at its darkest hour and oppose the man who he recognized as evil.

In the end, this is the knowledge that makes *The Cost of Discipleship* such an empowering and emotive read. Bonhoeffer really did do everything he possibly could to fulfil his beliefs in what Jesus would have wanted him to do. So much so that he died a truly miserable death as a result. So when we read this book we are getting a glimpse into the soul of someone who lived a genuinely admirable life in the most appalling of circumstances.

We may hope that the cost of our discipleship need not be as great, but at the same time the book forces us to consider what we would have done if we were in the place of Bonhoeffer. No one can truly know what they would do in those circumstances, but we can be grateful that there are people who had the courage and resolve to do the right thing in the face of evil.

The Cost of Discipleship

The Speed Read

Cheap grace is the characteristic of those who believe that they need not fully engage with Jesus to live a good life. But if we examine Christ's Sermon on the Mount it becomes apparent that he wanted us to commit heart and soul to him. We must experience the pain and suffering of sacrifice to achieve costly grace. We must do whatever it takes to be worthy of being his disciples in the world.

The Seven Storey Mountain, 1948
Thomas Merton

"The devil is no fool. He can get people feeling about heaven the way they ought to feel about hell. He can make them fear the means of grace the way they do not fear sin."

*T*HE *SEVEN STOREY MOUNTAIN* was written by the Trappist monk Thomas Merton at the age of 31. It is a remarkable account of his life, from an early rejection of religion, through conversion in his twenties, and on to his decision to withdraw into a monastery. The title is a reference to Dante's *Inferno*. The book has sold millions of copies since its publication in 1948. This is largely because of the compelling account it gives of the way in which the author decided to adopt a monastic lifestyle.

Merton was a natural writer. He was well educated and probably could have been successful in an academic career had he chosen to follow that path. His parents died in his youth and he had a complex childhood in which he moved between different homes in France, England, and then the United States. He had some religious teaching as a young man, but rejected its message declaring that he believed in nothing.

This nihilism led him to lead a relatively licentious life, drinking alcohol and indulging in casual sex. He describes himself at this age in the book as someone who is drifting, failing to find meaning in different areas such as literature and radical politics. Finally, he came back to the church, converting to Catholicism when he was 23.

He became a monk, living in the Cistercian Order at

Gethsemani Abbey in Kentucky. In spite of his confinement, he reported this as a moment when he finally realized his freedom. *The Seven Storey Mountain* gives an appealing picture of the peace and fulfillment that he found as a result of this withdrawal from the world.

The book is well written and compelling, but the scale of its success was something that was something of a surprise to the publishers. Why was it such a success?

We have to bear in mind that the period after the Second World War was a rather strange time, when people were deeply concerned about the threat of nuclear attack, and the world still seemed a rather dangerous place. For many the savagery of the war had left a feeling of angst and pointlessness. And *The Seven Storey Mountain* came as a real breath of fresh air into that environment. It described a simpler way of life, and one in which these confusions could be left behind.

It was reportedly an inspiration for many young people who chose to enter the priesthood or holy orders in that period, or at least to turn back to a more contemplative form of religion. The book has been compared to St Augustine's *Confessions*. In both books, a young man turns away from the worldly sins and pleasures of his youth to seek a more spiritual path. Indeed, the Catholic Church was initially rather concerned about Merton's descriptions of his behavior before he entered holy orders, and some of the passages concerning this period of his life were cut in response to those concerns.

Another concern that some felt about the book was the degree to which it lionized one very specific type of Catholic faith, in the process denigrating other Christian communities and non-Catholic paths. This is probably a valid criticism of the book, although one can also read it simply as expressing the enthusiasm of a monk for the path he has chosen, and take this as something that might inspire anyone, no matter what path they choose to try to find spiritual growth.

Merton himself went on to become a well-known author and thinker, and in some of his later work, he did acknowledge that he wouldn't have written the same book if he had written it at a later stage of his life. Indeed, his life continued to evolve as he aged – he became interested in leaving the Trappists for a less solitary order. And having hailed the virtues of living a life in pure contemplation, he ended up as a well-known figure, who traveled the world, rather than the silent monk that the book depicts. Merton would become a participant in the peace movement, and his later writing would take a broader view of spirituality than *The Seven Storey Mountain.*

However none of that detracts from the power of this book. It is a book that expresses a very particular point of view – that of a man in his thirties who has made a profound decision to turn away from a life of worldly success into private, religious contemplation and prayer. As such it has been an inspiration to many people. So while there may have been more to Thomas Merton, and to his life story than this single book, *The Seven Storey Mountain* survives as a powerful testament to one part of his journey.

The Seven Storey Mountain

The Speed Read

As a young man I was without direction, drifting from licentiousness to radical politics, from literature to academia without finding meaning. Then I converted to the Church and entered the Trappist monastery. There I found peace and fulfillment, and genuine freedom in spite of the four walls that surrounded me.

The Normal Christian Life, 1957
Watchman Nee

*"God makes it quite clear in His Word that He has only one
answer to every human need – His Son, Jesus Christ.
In all His dealings with us He works by taking us out of
the way and substituting Christ in our place."*

WATCHMAN NEE WAS a church leader who helped to spread Christianity around China in the first half of the twentieth century. He was imprisoned for his beliefs and acts in 1952 and spent the rest of his life in prison before his death in 1972.

He converted to Christianity in 1920 when he was 17 years old. He was strongly influenced by the British missionary M.E. Barber who taught him about many of the Christian classics of the past. Most of his learning came from direct study of the Bible and from reading the great books of predecessors who tried to explain their spiritual beliefs in writing. For 30 years Watchman Nee traveled around China helping to establish "local churches," institutions that he saw as indispensable in attempting to support the Christian faith.

He saw it as regrettable that people chose to separate the church of God into different denominations and hierarchies, arguing that the only legitimate way to create a smaller church was on a geographical basis – in other words it was natural for a community to have its own church. The local churches he founded became the bedrock of a Christian church that was widespread and strong at the time of the communist takeover in 1949.

During 1938 and 1939 Watchman Nee traveled to Europe and gave a series of talks – this later became the source material for *The Normal Christian Life,* which would be published in 1957. On the surface, the book is a commentary on the first few chapters of the New Testament book, *Romans.* The title is a reference to the question that the author starts with – "What is the normal Christian life?" Watchman Nee's contention is that the average Christian life today is not a normal one, but a subnormal one, which does not come up to the standards that God asks of us.

As a starting point for answering the question, he returns to the answer given by St Paul in Galatians, Chapter 2 – "It is no longer I, but Christ." Watchman Nee sees this as meaning that "I live no longer, but Christ lives His life in me." He wants us to live in Christ, to escape from fear and darkness by recognizing the great gift that God has given us, which consists of the forgiveness, absolution from sin, and the path toward the light which are embodied in Christ.

Watchman Nee is unflinching on the subject of sin. He confronts the problem of why even believers are still tempted by sin, but sees in Christ a way to get beyond this problem. He looks at what it means to live one's life in the holy spirit. Even though we should be able to leave sin and the problems of the flesh behind, we struggle to do so. So how can we see ourselves as being liberated in Christ's love?

The problem for Nee is that too many Christians try to live in themselves, in their own strength, and thus in their own feelings. What they need to do is "take their hands off," and put their faith in Christ. We fail because we do not let Christ into our lives, because we do not understand that God's gift to us was his son, and that the only true path is to live our lives in Christ.

In spite of the communist take-over, after which many of his fellow Christians escaped the mainland, Watchman Nee felt he had to stay in China and to continue with his work.

His leadership of the local churches inevitably led to him being treated as an enemy of the state. He was arrested in 1952. In 1956 he was finally sentenced to 15 years imprisonment. Only his wife was allowed to visit him in this time. His dignity through this persecution is one of the reasons that he is remembered as such an inspiration. His very last letter alluded to his suffering, but only in positive terms:

> *In my sickness, I still remain joyful at heart.*

Since his death in 1972, Watchman Nee's influence has persisted through a wide variety of different spiritual thinkers, and he is remembered for his own words in *The Normal Christian Life* and his many other publications and writings.

The Normal Christian Life

The Speed Read

The average Christian life is not the normal Christian life, the life that God would want us to live. Rather than trying to live in our own strength, we need to understand the great gift that God gave us in Christ, and live our lives through Christ. We live in a world of sin and the flesh, but we can escape from temptation by sacrificing ourselves to Christ.

Community and Growth, 1979
Jean Vanier

"I know that God has chosen the poor to astound the rich and the strong. I know that he loves me as I am, with my handicaps."

I N THE MODERN WORLD we are often confronted with a very particular opposition between the individual and society. Many political ideas revolve around the question of whether the individual or the state should be the focus of policy and moral agency. Such oppositions miss one of the most fundamental aspects of life which is that, before we live in a state or society, we live in a community.

In the work of Jean Vanier, we see someone who takes the idea of community with the seriousness it deserves. We also see a man who has created communities around the world which humble those of us who are too scared or too busy to take responsibility for the weakest members of our communities.

Vanier was the founder of the L'Arche movement, an international network of communities in which people from a variety of faith backgrounds live together with people with developmental and learning disabilities. The loving support these communities provide is in stark contrast to the institutions in which people with disabilities often had (and still have) to live in many parts of the world.

L'Arche is French for The Ark, as in the biblical story of Noah. Vanier, who had a background in the navy and in training for the priesthood created the roots of the organization in 1964. Inspired by his friendship with the Dominican priest Father Thomas

Philippe and by Val Fleuri, a home and workshop for men with disabilities, Vanier founded a small house in Trosly-Breuil in France. There he would live together with two of the men who he had encountered while they were living in a harsh institution near Paris.

Providing a home for these men was only the start of Vanier's journey: from these small beginnings the organization grew in size and influence over the years to the international network it has become today.

Vanier has written a number of books on his work and on the ideas that underpin them. One of the aspects of the L'Arche experience that is very clear in his writing is the admirable relationship he has with those who live there. Rather than patronizing them in any way, Vanier always emphasizes the degree to which this is a relationship of friends, not of helper and dependent. He goes further than friendship when he emphasizes how much the more able members of these communities can learn from the "disabled" members.

He has written that "the idea of living together was there from day one. The idea of living happily together, of celebrating and laughing a lot, came very quickly and spontaneously. When the idea of the poor educating us came, I don't know exactly. The words of St Vincent de Paul, 'The poor are our masters,' were always there, but when they became a reality is uncertain."

Before L'Arche, Vanier had taken a doctorate in philosophy, where he wrote on the subject of happiness, a term he defined as "loving and being loved." In books such as *Community and Growth*, it is his ability to describe the way in which such love and happiness grow from our interactions with others that shines through. For Vanier, all relationships are mutual – and all of us suffer from weaknesses – the strength he describes best is the strength we find in others, and in our relationships and community.

Community and Growth is about more than Vanier's experiences of L'Arche. It is a book written from deep Christian beliefs, but one that would be of interest to anyone who has pondered the basic moral problems of society. For Vanier, we are all a mixture of good and bad qualities, strength and weakness, light and dark. When we recognize our own weaknesses with humility and grace we are more able to be receptive to the strength and goodness that we find in others.

Some might be inspired by Vanier to think about how they can help in their community, some might even wish to emulate the writer and find a community such as those organized by L'Arche. But for many readers, the great value of his writing is the light he casts on the idea of living a good life. The modern catchphrase "What would Jesus do?" captures an age-old question: How can I live my life in a more Christlike manner?

Vanier doesn't pretend that this is an easy question, and he doesn't hide the difficulties of life in a community. He acknowledges that we are capable of hate as well as love, but sees forgiveness, humility, and a desire to help others as attributes that are fundamental to a good way of life.

In this respect, *Community and Growth* is relevant to us all, as we all (with very few exceptions) live in communities. We all struggle with relationships and friendships on a daily basis. We can all recognize the difficulties of living up to Christ's admonition to love one's neighbor. That Vanier presents a vivid example of how to do so with the utmost vigor and sincerity can only be an inspiration. *Community and Growth* is a beautiful, gentle book, a meditation on how to live, and a celebration of the things that we all have in common as human beings.

Community and Growth

The Speed Read

Jean Vanier is to be admired as the founder of L'Arche communities, where people of many faiths live together with people who are developmentally disabled. Community and Growth is a meditation on the ideas that underpin Vanier's spirituality – the ways in which humans can live together and support one another, finding love, happiness and mutual support and in the process living in as Christlike a manner as possible. An inspiration to all, not just to those who might be interested in living in such a community.

No Greater Love, 1979
Mother Theresa

"I don't think there is anyone who needs God's help and grace as much as I do. Sometimes I feel so helpless and weak. I think that is why God uses me. Because I cannot depend on my own strength, I rely on Him twenty-four hours a day."

THE PUBLIC PERCEPTION of Mother Theresa has in some respects been affected by recent revelations that she spent a large part of her life in a depressed condition, and feeling that she had been forsaken by her God. Some see this as undermining her saintliness, but one could equally argue that her continued devotion to the poor and needy in spite of such personal crises, make her achievements all the more remarkable.

Mother Theresa was an Albanian Roman Catholic nun, who set up the Missionaries of the Poor in Kolkata in India. The organization looked after those who suffered from poverty and sickness, and cared for orphans and the elderly. From its foundation in 1950, this determined, compassionate lady helped literally thousands of people over 45-year period. The Missionaries of the Poor set up missions in more than a hundred countries. She saved lives, gave people hope in dark and difficult times, and fed and cared for those were in the most desperate need. There have inevitably been cavils about some details of her life's work and beliefs, but it is impossible to contemplate her achievements without awe for what she was able to do with her life.

No Greater Love is a collection of her thoughts, and a glimpse into the mind of someone who put Jesus' admonitions to his followers to exercise charity and to care for the poor at the center of her life. As a Catholic, she views good works and sacrifice as central parts of the path to salvation, and it has to be acknowledged that we cannot all share either her level of devotion or self-sacrifice. But this is a deeply inspiring book in spite of this.

In the book she talks of her work as being an attempt to emulate or imitate Jesus, and to act as he would have wanted us to do. At one point she argues that "if our poor die of hunger, it is not because God does not care for them. Rather, it is because neither you nor I are generous enough."

Mother Theresa's mission put the care of the needy above the obligation to try to teach the Christian message. The catechism was taught in the missions, but as she explains, she was impressed by the fact that Jesus chose to feed the crowds before he tried to teach them. She was a great believer in the idea that actions speak louder than words, and the example of charity and love that was created by the missions was one of her greatest legacies.

In the book she recounts anecdotes about some of the people she encountered in the course of her charitable work. She talks with great compassion about a woman who gives her crippled son the name "Teacher of Love," and of a child who rejected the opportunity to live in one of her homes because he preferred to stay with the mother he loved, and live under a tree. Her conviction that "we must conquer the world not with bombs but with love" also shines through, and presents us with a wonderful example of someone who was able to improve the world through simple actions.

Some posthumously published letters of Mother Theresa made it clear that she had a very difficult spiritual life. She felt abandoned by her God, writing in distressing terms of the anguish she felt:

> *When I try to raise my thoughts to Heaven – there is such convicting emptiness that those very thoughts return like sharp knives & hurt my very soul. I am told God loves me – and yet the reality of darkness & coldness & emptiness is so great that nothing*

touches my soul. Did I make a mistake in surrendering blindly to the Call of the Sacred Heart?

In retrospect it is clear that Mother Theresa suffered from a long "dark night of the soul." It was St John of the Cross who gave us this term, which is generally understood to refer to believers who come to doubt their faith and to feel that they have been forsaken by Jesus or God. The truly extraordinary thing in the life of Mother Theresa is that she was able to persist in her charitable actions in spite of this inner turmoil.

It has been observed that those who suffer from such dark nights of the soul can have the greatest spiritual enlightenment. If they are able to continue to live a good life in spite of such doubts, then they have the experience of living life according to religious principle, not for the reward of feeling good because of those actions, but in spite of the emptiness that is engendered. So they are being good for goodness' sake, not for the spiritual rewards that are experienced by those who are not suffering from the dark night of the soul.

The dark night only lifted late in Mother Theresa's life, and one can only hope that she was then able to look back over her life with joy at her achievements. Her desire to please Jesus and to act as He would have wanted her to led her to do great things, and her self-sacrifice in spite of her private doubts should only increase our admiration for her in retrospect.

This is a beautiful little book, and one that contains gems of real wisdom. It is also a fine way to remember someone who lived out a genuinely Christian life, and was not deflected from the path of goodness by her uncertainties and perceived weaknesses.

No Greater Love

The Speed Read

God helps me because I am weak, so I rely on him every day. In our missions, we help people because people need to eat before they are able to learn. We should conquer the world with love, not with bombs. By giving people an example of a life that Jesus would commend, we are teaching the world about love. "Silence of the heart is necessary so you can hear God everywhere – in the closing of the door, in the person who needs you, in the birds that sing, in the flowers, in the animals."

Secular Texts

Secular Texts: Introduction

IN THIS SECTION WE have gathered together a selection of titles that are either about spirituality or spiritual in themselves but that can't strictly be regarded as religious books. In the case of William Blake *(Songs of Innocence and Experience)* and Fyodor Dostoevsky *(The Idiot)* the writing is from Christian points of view, but these are such idiosyncratic takes on religion that they seem almost to be an interrogation of spiritual belief rather than a statement of faith.

The Varieties of Religious Experience by William James and *Modern Man in Search of a Soul* by Carl Jung are two titles that take a psychological approach, attempting to understand what it is that we experience in matters of faith and what value spirituality has for us as human beings. Both contain some fascinating insights into the way our minds work, and both take a mostly sympathetic view of religion.

The last three books in this section are three very different pieces of fiction. On the surface, *The Little Prince* by Antoine de

Saint-Exupéry and *The Soul Bird* by Michal Snunit are books for children. However they are both books that have been enjoyed and treasured by adults as well as children and that pack a powerful emotional and spiritual message into a simple format. Neither takes a formal religious point of view, but both are books that can be inspirational for people in need of spiritual refreshment.

Meanwhile *Franny and Zooey* by J.D. Salinger is a far more obviously sophisticated book, a story of highly educated New Yorkers and their spiritual fascinations. It is included here for its sheer enthusiasm for a wide range of spiritual writing, from the sayings of Jesus and the Upanishads to books such as *The Way of A Pilgrim,* which forms a crucial element of the plot. There are of course many novels that deal with spiritual concerns so the choice of Dostoevsky and Salinger in this section can only seem somewhat arbitrary, but their presence, together with those of the two "books for children" can act as a reminder that spiritual messages are to be found in a wide variety of sources, some less obvious than others.

Songs of Innocence and Experience,
1789–94
William Blake

"In every cry of every Man,
In every Infant's cry of fear,
In every voice: in every ban,
The mind-forg'd manacles I hear."

S OMETIMES IT TAKES a true maverick thinker to challenge our religious assumptions and make us think about what we truly believe. William Blake was one such thinker. A mystic, poet, and artist, much of Blake's best work has a profoundly spiritual angle to it.

Blake was drawn to Christianity but was strongly opposed to all organized religion and to what he saw as the political hypocrisies of his time. His most creative period was in the shadow of the French Revolution – *Songs of Innocence* was published in 1789 as the revolution was underway, while *Songs of Experience* was written five years later when the revolution had clearly turned ugly and Blake's disillusionment with the cause showed in this more weary set of poems.

He wrote some extraordinary "prophetic works," using imagery from the Bible and elsewhere to convey his radical ideas. One of the most concentrated explanations of his ideas comes in *The Marriage of Heaven and Hell.* Here he mixes poetry and prose in a story that draws on predecessors such as Dante's *Inferno* and Milton's *Paradise Lost.* He pictures a meeting between a devil and an angel and their visits to one another's realms. For Blake the devil is not an evil character, indeed he uses him (and the "Proverbs of Hell") to make the point that the organized church has used ideas of religion for its own oppressive purposes.

So Blake pictures Hell as a place of subversive and creative energy. He describes energy as "eternal delight" and sees the Dionysian (wild or primal) energy of hell as something that challenges the oppressive system of formal churches. To a degree this is a political allegory but there is also a theological challenge in Blake's thinking. He is acknowledging the degree to which "Evil" is a construction that can be used to formalize those qualities that the establishment is most uncomfortable with.

He is also rejecting the mind/body dualism of most philosophy under which the organized church has tended to label the natural energy and will of the body as being innately wrong, and has focused on the purity of mind and soul. So for him Good comes to be (wrongly) identified as something that is passive and that always obeys Reason, while Energy is always rejected as being evil.

C.S. Lewis was sufficiently appalled by these kinds of ideas that he wrote *The Great Divorce* in response. However, one needn't agree with every aspect of Blake's thought to find his writing on these subjects fascinating and stimulating. And there is also great beauty in his poetry. *Songs of Innocence and Experience* is probably his greatest poetic achievement because it packs such emotion and profundity into such simple verse.

Songs of Innocence mostly consists of poems that focus on the simplicity and joy of the natural world. Such things as a shepherd's love for his flock, or the beauty of a new born baby become inspirations for Blake. In *The Lamb,* he provides a perfectly formed poem introducing us to the creator of the beauty, God, who also called himself a lamb.

Songs of Experience followed five years later. It gives a more clouded vision of the human condition. Blake wanders the streets of London, noting the misery and poverty of many of its inhabitants. Many of the poems echo themes from the first volume, but take a darker or at least less innocent view of the same subjects. Blake expresses his anger at the inequalities of his time, through poems on subjects that are universal enough to strike a chord today.

Blake hadn't lost faith in mankind. But the second set of poems did express the idea that innocence and experience are two "contrary states of the human soul." For Blake true innocence depended on the possibility of experience, and vice versa. While raging against a world in which people and children were kept poor and in which religious dogma was rated over simple Christian virtues such as love and mercy, he recognized that we all grow from a state of innocence to a state of experience and that this is a necessary part of life.

Some of Blake's beliefs are specific to his times. But others have been echoed in later strands of thought. One can see elements of psychoanalysis in the way that he believes that energy should not be repressed. And his belief in the importance of creativity and the dangers of oppression from organized religion have been taken on in different ways over different generations.

But the lasting value of *Songs of Innocence and Experience* probably comes from something far simpler. This is truly beautiful poetry that leads us to contemplate the basic aspects of human existence and what it means to have a soul. In spite of his doubts about the organized church, Blake conveys some of the basic truths of the Christian message – those of charity, love, and mercy, in particular.

There may not be a clear direction for a Christian way of life here, but there is a very clear picture of the form of the human soul. Through the poetry of Blake we see the world more clearly, and that is in itself a remarkable spiritual achievement.

Songs of Innocence and Experience

The Speed Read

Infant Joy (from *Songs of Innocence*)
"I have no name;
I am but two days old.
What shall I call thee?
I happy am,
Joy is my name."

Infant Sorrow (from *Songs of Experience*)
"My mother groan'd! My father wept.
Into the dangerous world I leapt.
Helpless, naked, piping loud;
Like a fiend hid in a cloud."

The Idiot, 1868
Fyodor Dostoevsky

". . . the essence of religious feeling has nothing to do with any reasoning or any crimes and misdemeanours or atheism; it is something entirely different and it will always be so . . ."

*T*HE *IDIOT* IS AN extraordinary novel, by a writer of genius. Fyodor Dostoevsky always wrote with great intensity and often spoke of matters of faith and reason in his novels. He doesn't convey a unified philosophical message in his work: the characters each speak with their own voices and represent different sides of an argument.

Dostoevsky has been described as an existentialist, and as a pessimist. In fact he is better described as a mystical Christian and a Russian nationalist. His life views were partly shaped by two major events. His father died while he was young, probably a victim of murder by his own servants. Later on he came close to being executed for treason. Cruelly he was led to the scaffold, and left blindfolded on the verge of death, before he was informed that the sentence had been commuted. Both of these events led him to think deeply about the nature of life and death, crime and punishment, and the condition of his beloved country Russia.

Several of his novels deal in depth with these issues. His greatest novel *The Brothers Karamazov* explicitly presents his internal conflicts between faith, reason, and licentiousness in the characters of the brothers and their father. It also presents us with the parable of the Grand Inquisitor, a tale through which an atheist questions the entire basis of the church and the degree to which it has sometimes

chosen control and eradication of free will over the original teachings of Jesus.

The Idiot is a fascinating story in a different way. The main
character, Prince Myshkin, has often been described as Christlike, because he approaches the obstacles in his life with such
purity and innocence. Dostoevsky sets up a complex plot in which
the Prince is thrown into the Russian society of his day. The
Prince is an epileptic (like the author), and has been abroad
seeking help with his illness.

He therefore comes into this society as an outsider, who takes
everyone at face value, as he cannot help but trust in their sincerity
and try to act toward them in a goodly manner. He shows a
genuine, touching Christian love for many of those whom he
encounters, and tries his best to help them, in spite of their deep
flaws and problems.

He is often mired in confusion and doubt himself, but it is
because he cannot tell how to retain his virtue in the face of such
moral complexities. In the end, the goodness of the Prince is not
sufficient to overcome the problems he is faced with, but he is
nonetheless an inspiring character.

In detail the plot concerns Prince Myshkin's friendship with
Rogozhin, a dark brooding character who is in love with Nastasya
Filipovna, a society woman of questionable virtue. Although the
Prince also comes to love another girl, Aglaya, he is drawn into a
form of love triangle with Rogozhin and Nastasya, as he proposes
to her in an attempt to save her from herself, out of a Christian
sense of duty to help a soul in torment.

As with all Dostoevsky books, this is a long dense read, although
there are many hilarious and emotionally involving scenes. From
the point of view of spirituality, the really fascinating passages
come in various meditations and conversations on the subject of
faith in reason, especially in some of the exchanges between the
licentious Rogozhin and the saintly Prince.

At the heart of the novel's religious message is a section on
which the Prince muses about a variety of recent experiences he
has had in which people have interacted with religion. First he

talks at length to a well known atheist on a train. He concludes that while this man is very learned and interesting, he is never truly addressing the issue he believes he is talking about. Something in his approach to atheism prevents him from truly understanding the nature of the simple faith of someone like the Prince.

Secondly he hears an anecdote about two peasants who are old friends. One of the friends covets an expensive watch that the other has obtained, and so cuts his throat to steal it, but he cannot bring himself to do this without first asking the Lord's forgiveness and crossing himself. Thirdly he is swindled by a beggar who sells him an obviously cheap tin cross, pretending it is silver. The prince is perfectly aware that is tin, but concludes that "I mustn't be too quick to condemn a man who has sold his Christ. God only knows what is locked away in these weak and drunken hearts."

Finally he tells the lovely story of a young peasant girl who he has seen crossing herself after seeing her baby smile. He asks her why and she responds:

> *Well sir, just as a mother rejoices seeing her baby's first smile, so does God rejoice every time he beholds from above a sinner kneeling down before Him to say his prayers with all his heart.*

Myshkin comments that this is one of the most beautiful, profound things he has ever heard and that the young peasant girl has expressed the fundamental idea of Christianity. In this short sequence of disparate experiences, Dostoevsky manages to pack in an incredible amount of profound thought about the religious experience and the paradoxes it can engender.

It is in passages like this that Dostoevsky's passionate spirituality shines through. He never presents the reader with simple solutions or with a packaged set of opinions. Instead he asks searching questions of his characters, and subjects them to impossible dilemmas as part his investigation into what faith and reason can achieve in the modern world. But by treating his characters in this way, he reveals a huge amount about the religious experience, and shows us a variety of different ways in which we might choose to lead a spiritual life.

Prince Myshkin is also one of the most lovely and tragic figures in literature. His take on Christianity is so simple and open-hearted, that even when he gets himself into irredeemable tangles and difficulties, we can only love him in spite of everything. Seeing that the author clearly loves his characters also leads the reader to see Christian love from new angles, and in the end this is the real subject of this book.

The Idiot

The Speed Read

Prince Myshkin, a partially healed epileptic, returns from abroad. Befriending Rogozhin, a worldly, difficult man who loves Nastasya Filipovna, he is drawn into a situation of escalating difficulties. He attempts throughout to deal with this with Christian love, curiosity, and innocence. Even though he is not able to resolve all the problems he faces, he provides an inspiring and intriguing character, through which we are led to interrogate the nature of faith and reason.

The Varieties of Religious Experience, 1902

William James

*"Be not afraid of life. Believe that life is worth living
and your belief will help create the fact."*

WILLIAM JAMES' writing on religion is about the subject of spirituality, more than it is spiritual in and of itself. But it is nonetheless well worth reading for anyone with an interest in spiritual matters, for the light it casts on psychological aspects of religion and prayer.

James was a multi-talented thinker, who published work in many fields other than religion, including physiology, psychology, and philosophy. With Charles Sanders he was known as a founder of the philosophical movement pragmatism. This was the theory that knowledge can only be judged on its practical results in the world – that the usefulness of a belief can be of more significance than whether or not it is possible to prove that belief true beyond all possible doubt. This is of course an idea that is of interest to someone who believes that their religious faith is an indispensable virtue in a world of doubt, whether or not the existence of God can be proven.

James grew up in an intellectual, liberal household. His father was a theologian, and his sister and brother were both skilled writers (his brother Henry was the well known novelist). He had a successful academic career, graduating from Harvard and going on to teach there. However he had a lifelong tendency to depression and melancholy. This became one of the factors that fed into his fascination with spirituality.

At the heart of James' writing was his thinking about conscious-ness and truth. He was unusual amongst philosophers in that he explicitly recognized the fact that many thinkers, while claiming to search for objective truth, end up producing work that suits their own prejudices and desires rather than being pure reflections of truth.

This idea, that writers are often more subjective than they realize, was carried into his writing on religious belief. At times he claimed that religion was something that science couldn't penetrate, that it was something that people could only approach on an individual basis. But at other times, he wrote that it was possible for a study of human nature to help us to achieve a more scientific understanding of the religious experience.

In 1890 James published his massive book *Principles of Psychology*. This did much to establish the foundations of psychology as a serious, modern science. He argued that the introspective study of our own minds could help us to comprehend how the mind works. He talked about the "stream of consciousness" of the human mind, and argued that as well as understanding how the mind worked we could perceive that we acted with free will.

This provided the foundation for his later writing on religious belief. In *The Will To Believe* (1897) he applied his pragmatic ideas to spirituality. He considered the idea that it is the consequences of believing that are most important in a religious context. He saw belief in terms of individual choices, and defended the idea that we can rationally choose to believe in some propositions, although we know they lie beyond the realm of provable truth.

Pragmatism was a form of verificationism, in which the meaning of a statement is judged by the consequences of believing it. Other verificationists and pragmatists would use their method to reject all metaphysical beliefs, including those of religion. James was a far more subtle thinker, and rather than rejecting metaphysics, he chose to try to define and understand the way that we choose to believe in metaphysical and religious statements, in spite of our lack of certainty.

It is in *The Varieties of Religious Experience* (1902) that James best sums up his philosophy of religion. Since Pascal's wager, philosophers had played with the idea that one might choose to believe in God in the spirit of a gamble, on the basis that the consequences of being wrong are worse for the person who chooses atheism than for the person who chooses belief. For most believers this is a very unsatisfactory compromise as it implies that one believes not out of faith but out of fear.

Up to a point James' writing can be used to justify religious belief in the same way as Pascal's wager did. However there is more to his view of spiritual experiences. He sees truth as being defined by the personal consequences of belief rather than by how accurately it describes an external reality. So in his thinking, we can judge how useful (and thus true) a belief in God is by judging its consequences in our life. If we can clearly see that a belief in God leads to better outcomes, then we can judge it to be a useful or true belief.

Of course, one can debate what a "better outcome" is forever, but on purely ethical grounds, many believers would argue that having God in their lives leads them to live better lives. And for James this is an important thing, not to be sneered at as many philosophers would.

James makes some other important points about religion. He looks at the case of the Quaker religion and its founder George Fox. Many modern observers believe that Fox was schizophrenic. For the scientists and philosophers who were James' primary audience, this would be a reason to reject his beliefs. However James firmly points out that the origin of a belief is of no consequence when we try to study its value or truth.

He also looks more closely at the idea that religious belief can have real consequences in our lives. He castigates scientists for their tendency to ignore the "real, physical" consequences of unseen objects and symbols. He talks about how the word "steak" on a menu or the thought of a lemon can cause us to salivate. In the same way religious beliefs may have real consequences, so even though traditional science finds it hard to explain those consequences, it would be unwise to reject them per se.

He also makes an interesting contrast between the healthy mind and the sick soul. Some of his writing on this point is very much of its time, and modern readers may take issue with his idea that some people are just "naturally happy". However he does give a convincing picture of different types of people, who we might call optimists and pessimists. The sick souls find it hard to find the good in anything, while the healthy-minded naturally enjoy life and look for the best in any situation.

Possibly thinking of his own depression, James ponders the idea that sick souls can only be cured through a mystical experience. This foreshadowed Jung's later ideas on the same point, ideas that would feed into the founding of Alcoholics Anonymous. For James, "twice born" souls, those who have been sick but have been cured by a spiritual epiphany, may be the ones who end up most healthy and happy in the end, since they understand life from both persepectives.

This is a possible explanation and justification of the fervor of those in the evangelical movement who feel that they have been born again. But for many who have found consolation and release in religious belief James' writing on this point will strike a chord.

One doesn't read James on religion for spiritual inspiration. But if one approaches his writing for what it is – an investigation into the psychology of religious belief – one can find many valuable insights. And his understanding of the truth and value of spirituality is an unusually sensitive one among scientists and philosophers. By finding ways to justify religion and ethics in a pragmatic, philosophical way, James allows us to see that is not only possible, but hugely valuable to seek spiritual truth, rather than only granting something value if it is recognized by the pure rationalism of science.

The Varieties of Religious Experience

The Speed Read

The truth and usefulness of a statement depends on its consequences in our lives. We cannot reject ideas merely because of their origins, or because they rely on "unseen factors." Religious belief can have genuine consequences in life. Healthy souls look for the good in everything, while sick souls suffer from negativity and depression. But a sick soul cured by a spiritual experience can be the healthiest of all souls as it has been "born twice."

Modern Man in Search of a Soul, 1933
Carl Jung

"The least of things with a meaning is worth more in life than the greatest of things without it."

K NOWN PRIMARILY as a psychoanalyst, Carl Jung is also a fine writer when it comes to matters of spirituality. His writing on the subject comes fundamentally from the viewpoint of an investigation into man's need for spirituality, but this leads him to some intriguing insights. *Modern Man in Search of a Soul* is a useful introduction to his writing on this subject. It is a series of essays, written for the layman rather than the expert psychiatrist, which analyze the need of the average person need to search for their soul.

Jung was a Freudian and a close friend of Sigmund Freud, but their friendship suffered a notorious split in 1913. Jung suffered from some kind of breakdown in the next few years, and a great deal of his subsequent work dealt with his own mental condition during this difficult period. This is one of the aspects of his writing that gives it a direct appeal to the modern reader.

It is also interesting that Jung was fascinated by a range of subjects that some might now regard as somewhat mystical, ranging from myths, Arthurian legend, and flying saucers to Eastern philosophy. But in many of these cases his interest was partly in what drives the human mind to seek meaning in the world around us. He is interested in such subjects for their own sake, and also for the way in which they allow us to explore the psyche.

Jung was also intrigued by the unconscious. While Freud saw it as a place where our primitive selves resided, something which we struggled to repress, Jung saw it as a potential source of creativity, and the source of the friction that leads us toward the process of psychological individuation.

He also spoke often of the "collective unconscious." This idea shouldn't be understood to mean that people have some kind of shared mind. Instead it means that human beings share so much with one another in terms of experience, understanding, sensory capacity, and so on, that we have a similar mental set-up.

At times in Jung's writing he tries to understand how this leads us to create myths for our societies, and in this respect he treats religion as one myth among others. But at the same time, he sometimes spoke of a personal belief in God and religion, and he regarded spirituality as being of great importance regardless.

An interesting anecdote concerns his role in inspiring the 12 steps program popularized by Alcoholics Anonymous. He was treating an American patient (known as Rowland H.) who suffered from problems with alcohol. Jung told him of his belief that only a spiritual experience could reform an alcoholic.

Rowland managed to conquer his drinking problem after taking this advice, and returning to the United States to join an evangelical Christian group. This story came to the attention of Bill Wilson, who in turn managed to conquer his drinking problem and went on to co-found the AA.

Clearly Jung's influence was somewhat secondhand on the program. But the important part of his teaching that made its way through into the final 12-step program was the idea that a spiritual experience can lead us to transform our selves. Just as we go through a process of individuation and create a "self" in which we believe, a spiritual experience can lead us to reform or revise this self at a later date.

In his study of religions ranging from Christianity to Taoism and Gnosticism to Buddhism, Jung saw a common thread in this kind of journey of self transformation. He saw the religion as a journey to find the self and at the same time to search for the Divine. He also regarded spiritual experience as being essential to our well being and even sanity.

In *Modern Man in Search of a Soul*, the essays lay out an overview of Jung's psychological theories. He writes interestingly about dream analysis, symbols, the purpose of psychotherapy, the formation of personality, and life stages. He also contrasts "modern man" with the "archaic man." In his view, the true modern man is one who has taken on board all the modern viewpoints, and who relies on logic and science rather than on unconscious instinct and spirituality. He contrasts this with the relative simplicity of Archaic Man's lifestyle and belief system.

He doesn't make the mistake of saying that one is necessarily the better man, but he points out that modern man suffers from spiritual unease, possibly because he has become too detached from his unconscious instincts. Jung's time in India had left him fascinated with Eastern religion, and also led him to believe that having a greater appreciation of the unconscious, and integrating spirituality into everyday life would lead to a healthier mindset. He argues that modern man needs to move back toward values such as faith, love, and insight.

In the last essay in *Modern Man in Search of a Soul*, Jung makes a comparison between psychotherapists and priests. He says that while priests may not know as much about the scientific study of the mind, they do know a great deal about those values which are so necessary for the soul. He believed that many people became psychically unwell, or at least suffered from angst later in middle age and beyond because they lost their religious outlook, and their modern outlook prevented them from seeking spiritual assistance, whether it be from a priest or other source.

In the end this is possibly the most important message to be taken from this interesting book. Jung believed in the science of psychotherapy and in its ability to comprehend the unconscious mind. But he also recognized the fact that analysis alone was not enough to help with our spiritual unease. We need balance and harmony, and sometimes science and logic are not the solution – instead we need to return to a more spiritual response to life's challenges and problems.

Modern Man in Search of a Soul

The Speed Read

Through dreams and symbols, through mysticism and myths, we can trace the unconscious need for meaning and purpose in man's life. Religion is a journey of self transformation, in which we discover ourselves. Deep spiritual experiences can lead us to develop and grow. Modern man has gained much, but he has also lost contact with his instincts and unconscious. As a result he often suffers from spiritual unease, and the modern mindset sometimes prevents him from seeking religious remedies for this. Science and logic teach us a great deal but sometimes they are not enough. Instead we need to return to the simpler values of faith, love, and trust in our unconscious.

The Little Prince, 1943
Antoine de Saint-Exupéry

"One sees clearly only with the heart.
Anything essential is invisible to the eyes."

*T*HE LITTLE PRINCE is a children's book, but it is one that can be a spiritually rewarding read for adults as well. It is a simple fable about the friendship between a pilot who has crashed in the desert and the little prince he meets there. The author, Antoine de Saint-Exupéry, was himself a keen aviator. He flew airplanes for freight companies in North Africa and South America in the pre-war period, having several crashes of his own. Once he crashed in the Sahara and had to walk for several days to reach safety, and this was the inspiration for *The Little Prince.*

The book starts with the pilot, who has crash-landed in the desert. We learn that the pilot became disillusioned with the adults in his life while he was a child, as he discusses their failure to realize that a picture he drew of a snake that has eaten an elephant was not just a picture of a hat.

He finds "serious people" and adults lacking in something that comes naturally to children. One might call this innocence or open mindedness. Either way, the quality he dislikes in adults is their inability to approach the world and understand it for its own sake, and the failure to use their imagination and intuition.

At this stage of the story the pilot encounters a young boy in the desert, who is actually a little prince who has come to earth from a miniature planet far away. We don't find this out straight away. The pilot and prince have a series of absorbing and playful conversations. On the prince's planet he has several volcanoes and a single flower, with whom he is in love. He has become sad about this relationship and has run away from home.

He travels to a series of planets where he meets some strange people, including an alcoholic, a businessman who sees the world only in term of money, a king with no one to rule over, and a lamplighter who keeps lighting and putting out the lights on his planet for no apparent reason.

In each of their ways these characters display a kind of spiritual emptiness. They are obsessed only with one way of valuing the world and fail to see it from a more innocent point of view. The prince sees them all as being rather strange, from his childish viewpoint.

Finally he reaches our world where he meets a snake, and visits a garden where he realizes that his flower, who he thought so unique, is actually one of many roses. He also meets a fox, who becomes his pet, but this means that both of them are saddened when they have to part. These encounters feed into the prince's meditations on the strangeness of love, and the way that our attachments to other people are capable of causing us great pain.

However this also teaches the prince that his love for the flower is a special one, even though she is not the unique being he imagined. The bond between them has grown from the reality that he has cared for her and looked after. The insights into love and the way that love can grow between people are one of the book's most intriguing, if ambiguous elements.

A large part of the appeal of the book lies in the way that it contrasts the adult and child's point of view. At one stage the prince talks about the way that adults perceive a house:

> *If you tell grown-ups, "I saw a beautiful red brick house, with geraniums at the windows and doves on the roof . . . ," they won't be able to imagine such a house. You have to tell them, "I saw a house worth a hundred thousand francs." Then they exclaim, "What a pretty house!*

He also talks often of the way that people should see with their heart instead of with their minds. The prince is a beautiful character, someone who sees everything in life from a completely fresh point of view. Many of his observations on the strangeness of human and adult behavior can be applied to all of us. The book reminds us of a simpler time in our life, when we used our childish imaginations to reconstruct the world around us, rather than viewing the world through received ideas and prior notions.

The emotional nature of the story may occasionally mean that what appears to be spiritual insight is in fact less than profound than a first reading would suggest. But there are some genuine insights in this little book. In the taming of the fox, the prince realizes that the important things in our lives often develop over long periods through emotional attachments. He also comes to see that love transforms its object – that by loving something or someone, one brings meaning to the world and elevates the existence of both the lover and the loved.

This is something that will strike a chord with anyone who has pondered the nature of love in religious practice, as well as with those who have thought hard about the words of St Paul in 1 Corinthians 13:

> *When I was a child, I talked like a child, I thought like a child, I reasoned like a child. When I became a man, I put childish ways behind me. Now we see but a poor reflection as in a mirror; then we shall see face to face. Now I know in part; then I shall know fully, even as I am fully known. And now these three remain: faith, hope and love. But the greatest of these is love.*

Antoine de Saint-Exupéry focuses on the idea that to think and reason like a child is to return to that innocent part of our nature which we have lost. Many of the adults in the book are seen as foolish or pointless, but in the narrator, the pilot, he presents a character who can care for the prince with the same care as that which a parent might feel for a child, but who is also still in touch with his own inner child.

The great value of this book is the way that it makes us think about our own lives and the way that we deal with being "grown up." If we have lost the ability to see the world as a child, or to love as a child does, then perhaps we are worse off as a result. But in the end it is more important to retain some of the aspects of innocence as we grow to be adults, and to be able to love and understand the world from an adult point of view as well.

The Little Prince

The Speed Read

A pilot crashes in the desert. There he meets a little prince, a beautiful innocent who has traveled across the stars, learning about the foolishness of human nature. Through their friendship, both learn more about the nature of love. To perceive the world only as an adult and to lose the ability to see the world as a child can rob us of one of the most important aspects of being a human.

Franny and Zooey, 1961
J.D. Salinger

*"I'm just sick of ego, ego, ego. My own and everybody else's.
I'm sick of everybody that wants to get somewhere, do something
distinguished and all, be somebody interesting. It's disgusting."*

THE WRITER J.D. Salinger is best known for his hugely successful novel of adolescent angst, *The Catcher in the Rye.* There are moments of spirituality in that book, but the author's interest in mysticism and religious ideas is far more explicit in his books about the Glass family: *Franny and Zooey, Raise High the Roofbeam, Carpenters and Seymour: An Introduction.* All of these books deal with members of a hyper-intelligent New York clan. The children have each appeared on a radio talk show as precocious youths and, under the influence of their brilliant eldest brother Seymour, are conversant in a wide range of philosophy, theology, and spirituality.

The result is a fascinating series of books in which serious ideas about Zen, psychology, and the meaning of prayer are casually dropped into the intellectual but entertaining stories. By the last story, *Seymour: An Introduction,* there is barely even a story to break up the spiritual observations, but the earlier *Franny and Zooey,* which introduced the family has more of a narrative drive.

Franny and *Zooey* were originally two separate stories, published in the New Yorker. In the shorter *Franny,* the protagonist Franny Glass visits New Haven, meeting up with her student boyfriend Lane with whom she is to attend the Yale football match and a party. Franny is carrying the Russian book *The Way of a Pilgrim.* In this religious work, an anonymous monk travels across the countryside, studying the *Philokalia* (a collection of Eastern Orthodox texts) and using a prayer rope as part of his constant practice of the "Jesus Prayer" ("Lord Jesus Christ, Son of God, have mercy on me, a sinner").

Franny has become fascinated by the idea that one should recite the Jesus prayer constantly, so that it synchronizes with our breathing and heartbeat, in order to achieve a state of constant mindfulness of Jesus. She contrasts this with the shallow self-obsession of the college life, personified in Lane's self-absorption and literary pretentiousness. She has become tired of the constant striving for status and self-importance that she perceives around her.

As a result she has quit a play that she was supposed to be acting in, having become distressed by the idea the she has been "acting fake" all the time. She also seems somewhat disturbed, refusing to eat, becoming faint and retreating to the restroom, where she starts to feverishly read her book. On emerging, she parts company with Lane and it becomes apparent that she has started to recite the prayer under her breath.

Zooey picks up the story a couple of days later. Franny's pursuit of the Jesus Prayer has turned into an emotional collapse. She has retreated to her mother's apartment in Manhattan and is refusing to discuss her breakdown with anyone. What she really wants is to speak to the eldest brother Seymour, who killed himself while on vacation years before.

Franny is the youngest of the family, and Zooey is her nearest brother in age, a successful actor. The two of them both respect eldest brothers Seymour and Buddy, but feel that they were raised almost as an experiment with the eldest brothers filling them with ideas about their spiritual and philosophical heroes.

The story begins with Zooey taking a long bath, interrupted by his mother, during which he rereads a letter from his brother Buddy, which reveals some of this family history. After arguing with his mother, he attempts to talk to Franny, who is in the living room, refusing to leave the sofa. Zooey interrogates Franny as to what she is trying to achieve by reciting the Jesus prayer, but she becomes infuriated by what she sees as his presumptuous and condescending approach. He feels he has failed to help her.

He retreats to the bedroom of the eldest brothers' bedroom, where he spends some time reading a sheet of paper that is tacked to the back of the door, on which the two brothers have noted down some of their favorite quotes from their reading. Salinger's own interests come shining through in the authors referenced, which range from Eastern religious texts such as the Upanishads and the Japanese poet Issa, to less obvious spiritual sources such as Ring Lardner and Franz Kafka.

In some respects this is the spiritual center of the two stories as we get a glimpse into a search for meaning that has ranged across such disparate texts in search of an answer to the apparent meaninglessness of modern life.

Franny's breakdown is clearly caused by a kind of existential angst about the inauthenticity of life, and the impossibility of achieving spiritual satisfaction. Her retreat to the Jesus Prayer is both infuriating (in its simplicity) and impressive, in the way that one might be impressed by the life of a genuine monk or nun. There is also a feeling in the book that this is something of a youthful moment of dilettantism, but that it is underpinned by powerful feelings of angst nonetheless.

After reading his brothers wallchart and reorienting his thoughts, Zooey decides to have one last attempt at talking to his sister. However having upset her previously, he decides to do this via the persona of their brother Buddy, who has been hard to contact. Impersonating him, he places a call to Franny, who not knowing that the call is fake and coming from just down the hall, takes it in their parents' bedroom.

"Buddy" starts by listening to her gripes about Zooey, and then they discuss her situation. After a while the mask slips and Franny realises that it is in fact Zooey. She is initially angry but they continue to talk, and this time the conversation goes more deeply into the philosophical and religious underpinning of Franny's angst.

Salinger was fascinated by the Zen idea of "satori," a mystical moment during which one achieves a new understanding of a spiritual problem. The quotes on the back of elder brothers' door are an example of the way that he looks for inspiration in both spiritual masters such as Meister Eckhart and in far more mundane sources. In *Seymour: An Introduction,* he spends several pages elaborating on the idea that one can find a moment of spiritual insight from something as simple as a game of marbles played on the curb.

Franny and Zooey is largely about the search for such a moment of spiritual insight. In the end Zooey is able to achieve what he has previously failed to do and communicates something about his understanding of Seymour's thought to Franny. This unlocks the problems she is undergoing and she is able to achieve a peaceful resolution to her breakdown, thanks to Zooey's spiritual assistance.

It is certainly possible to find J.D. Salinger's writing somewhat pretentious and self-indulgent. The mystical nature of his later work, combined with his eventual retreat from public life (he refused to publish anything after the combined publication of *Raise High the Roofbeam, Carpenters* and *Seymour: An Introduction* in 1963) gave him the reputation of being something of a reclusive guru. The 1960s fascination with eastern religion and existentialism maybe helped to create an aura around him as a writer that dissipated only slowly over the years.

However, the books do have an enduring appeal and can be seen as genuinely inspiring from a spiritual point of view. They achieve two particular things. Salinger's fascination in spiritual texts is apparent throughout the stories, and in many cases people have been inspired to investigate the original texts after reading his rather unique take on them. The sheer enthusiasm of the Glass family for books such as *The Way of a Pilgrim* or *The Cloud of Unknowing* make one want to know more about the original sources.

Secondly, the Glass family represent a way of living that might be somewhat hyper-intellectual, but nonetheless takes spirituality and mindfulness as central questions. The family have detailed discussions of religion and philosophy on an everyday basis, and the stories show various members in moments of spiritual crisis and resolution. By making the idea that we should be unembarrassed about spirituality and indeed make it a central part of our lives, Salinger gives us a flawed but inspiring example of a different way of approaching life.

Franny and Zooey

The Speed Read

Franny, youngest sister in a family of New York child geniuses, doesn't want to be fake anymore. She suffers a spiritual breakdown and tries to console herself with constant repetition of the simple Jesus Prayer, following the example of the Russian wanderer in *The Way of a Pilgrim*. Her nearest brother Zooey contemplates her problem and attempts to help, appealing to spiritual texts of the past and their mutual relationship with their eldest siblings, who tried to teach them to live a life of mindfulness.

Franny finally gets some sleep.

The Soul Bird, 1998
Michal Snunit

"Deep down,
inside our bodies,
lives the soul.
No one has ever seen it,
but we all know it's there."

BOOK NEEDN'T be a difficult or heavy read to be a spirtual experience. We can find inspiration in simple things as well as in more complex ideas. Many everyday experiences such as someone expressing a profound opinion on talk radio or the internet, the books we read to our children, the simple prayers we remember from childhood, and the stories we hear on the news can be as inspiring as the most dense religious texts.

One small example is *The Soul Bird,* by Michal Snunit. This is a very short, illustrated book that can be enjoyed by children or adults. It contains less than 1,000 words, but it can be a source of great wisdom and consolation.

Michal Snunit is an Israeli who was brought up on a kibbutz. She worked within the kibbutz system and also as a journalist, songwriter, and magazine editor. Her book is a poetic description of the "soul bird" who lives inside us all. Starting out by reminding us that we all have a soul, even if we are not in daily contact with it, she goes on to talk about how the soul reacts when we have various emotional experiences.

One of the powerful aspects of this short book is the way that it honestly faces up to our shortcomings and problems as human beings. She talks about how the soul bird feels when we are angry, jealous or miserable. She also imagines that the soul bird has a series of drawers to which it has the key. These include drawers for our innermost secrets, but also places where we hide away our anger, joy and sorrows.

In conclusion, the book suggests that we don't listen to our soul bird often enough, that some of us only hear it once in a lifetime. The remedy is that we should try, maybe late at night, or at another time of peace and quiet, to hear the voice of the soul bird, and listen to what it is telling us.

The book has been compared to *The Little Prince,* that other masterpiece of simplicity and emotion, but it is an even simpler text. However it manages to wrap quite a deep emotional punch into its spare and direct language. We all know that we sometimes hide things from ourselves, that we can be subject to self deceptions and confusions. And we all know too that there are moments in life where we feel that we have truly managed to be in touch with our own souls.

By finding a way to express these difficult emotional ideas so beautifully, Michal Snunit clearly struck a chord with many readers. *The Soul Bird* is a hugely popular book, which has been translated into more than 25 languages, and sold 400,000 copies in her native Israel alone.

Sometimes in life the consolation and encouragement we need can be found in small, everyday places, and *The Soul Bird* is a lovely book for those moments when one is feeling in need of spiritual refreshment.

The Soul Bird

The Speed Read

Deep inside us is our soul bird. We know that it is there but we don't always hear its voice. When someone is unkind to us, our soul bird is in pain. When someone loves or hugs us, our soul bird reacts joyfully. The soul bird has many drawers, and it guards the key to them. Inside are our secret emotions and thoughts. We can't always open the drawers but the soul bird always has the key. Sometimes when it is quiet we should try to hear its voice.

Alternative Approaches

Alternative Approaches: Introduction

THERE ARE A myriad of different types of spirituality and religion, and it is impossible to do justice to them all in a book of this sort. Rather than even try, this section can best be seen as a rather eclectic grab bag of different books that might be of interest to anyone who cares about spiritual matters.

Several of the books included here are fictions that address spiritual matters, including *Siddhartha* by Hermann Hesse and *The Prophet* by Kahlil Gibran. *The Teachings of Don Juan* by Carlos Castaneda is a more ambiguous case as some have suggested it is fiction, while it claims to be true. The doubts over its authenticity are at least a reminder that not all spiritual gurus are to be trusted.

There are also several primary texts from religious history included, in the *Tao Te Ching, Letters on the Sufi Path,* and *Spiritual Couplets.* D.T. Suzuki's *Essays in Zen Buddhism* had such a formative impact on the West's view of Zen that it almost deserves to be seen as a religious text in its own right.

Finally two books from the late twentieth century, *Be Here Now* by Ram Dass and *The Power of Now* by Eckhart Tolle are representative of the ongoing search for spiritual meaning in the modern age. While some of the new age attitudes and self-help manuals can be criticized for their shallow content, there are many thinkers and writers in the modern era who have gone through their own spiritual trials and tribulations and can be acknowledged to have made genuine contributions to the spiritual literature of the world.

Tao Te Ching, 6th Century BC (approx.)
Lao Tzu

"The Way that can be told of is not an unvarying way;
The names that can be named are not unvarying names.
It was from the Nameless that Heaven and Earth sprang."

S OME ANCIENT religious texts are notably difficult reads for those not expert in the relevant religion. But there are also ancient texts that retain a beauty and fascination even for those who can't follow every turn of the thought presented in the book. The *Tao Te Ching* falls into the latter category. It is over two millennia old, but it is a book of such ambiguous and beguiling wisdom that it makes for intriguing study for a modern Western reader.

Its detailed history is uncertain. It is reputed to be the work of Lao Tzu, but it is uncertain whether he was a real person, and the fact that his name can be translated as Old Master or Old Masters casts more doubt on the real source. The name Tao Te Ching is also ambiguous in translation, but approximately the words mean Way-Virtue-Classic Book/Scripture. Essentially this is a book of mystical and everyday wisdom, which centers on the idea of the Tao, or the Path – it was the classic on which Taoism was founded and thus also a major influence on Chinese Buddhism.

It is not a long book. It is organized into 81 short chapters, in which epigrammatic verses of wisdom are contained. It can be quite laconic, even funny at times, and can also be quite ambiguous. Even scholars of the Tao take different meanings from different sections due to its terse, poetic nature. But for all that, it can be a fascinating read.

The general framework of the book is based on a kingdom that is in a state of disorder and a consideration of what action or inaction would be undertaken by a wise ruler to restore harmony. The idea of the Tao is something that precedes man – the book considers an age of man prior to civilization and discusses the way that the Tao has developed and guided man. In its story of the creation, the *Tao Te Ching* refers to a genesis in which heaven and earth arise from an eternal, mysterious female. Heaven and earth come from the nameless and "the named is but the mother that rears the ten thousand creatures, each after its kind."

The *Tao Te Ching* contains an early version of the Chinese idea of oppositions: yin and yang, male and female. Many of its formulations refer to the rhythm of life, or the river of life that flows through the universe. So the spiritual path is identified as the search for harmony between opposing principles: day and night, mountain and river-valley, hot and cold.

A repeated theme in the book is the idea of returning:

> *In Tao the only motion is returning;*
> *The only useful quality, weakness.*
> *For though all creatures under heaven are the products of being,*
> *Being itself is the product of Not-being.*

Life arises from death, but there is a constant return to the eternity of death. This line of thought leads on to a typically oriental fascination with the relationship between form and nothingness. The Tao talks of the way that the usefulness of a wheel depends on the space in between the spokes. In terms of wisdom, it also talks about the idea that correct decisions arise from forgetting wisdom and trusting to the Tao. In a similar vein the book advises against "trying too hard" counseling that only be setting aside want and ambition can one succeed. This relates to the Buddhist idea of trying to achieve a state of emptiness and acceptance of the flow of the world:

Embracing the Way, you become embraced;
Breathing gently, you become newborn;
Clearing your mind, you become clear;
Nurturing your children, you become impartial;
Opening your heart, you become accepted;
Accepting the world, you embrace the Way.

But the book doesn't focus purely on mystical ideas such as these. It discusses the value of self knowledge and deals with ethical issues. Early Christian missionaries to China were attracted to the Tao by some of the surface similarities to Christian ideas – the *Tao Te Ching* advises us to requite injuries with good deeds, which has an obvious resemblance to the teaching of Jesus. The idea of the Tao has also sometimes been compared to the idea of the Word of God, though this may be groping too hard for resemblances between the two religions.

There are far more obvious relationships between the Tao and Eastern religious thought in Buddhism and Confucianism. In many respects, the *Tao Te Ching* expresses the ancient philosophy and wisdom from which those other religions drew breath. When reading the Tao, one cannot always clearly understand the meaning of the text. But there is always the sense that this is a crystallization of centuries of wisdom that has been passed down through generations.

In this respect it is also interesting to compare this text to the even earlier *I Ching* (Book of Changes). While the latter is most often used as a book of divination, it can also be read as a collection of advice on how to live one's life. Both books have a pure simplicity in their expression that reveals ever greater levels of complexity as one ponders the meanings of the texts – they also both address themselves to the problems of rulers, but can be taken as general advice for any individual. Both books are also subject to extremely variable translations – the lack of exact congruence between the logic of Chinese and English means that translation of such poetic and terse texts is a difficult and creative task.

Reading the *Tao Te Ching*, one can react in a number of different ways. The first is to see this as a historical document, a record of attitudes that developed in an ancient culture and that provide and insight into the mindset of that culture. The second is to take this purely as a book of condensed wisdom, from which we can find advice and guidance today. And finally one can simply read this as poetic book of spiritual observations, in which case it can lead one to meditate on the subjects discussed and to observe our own reaction to these ancient texts.

Whichever way one chooses to read the book, it is one that is worth repeated reads, no matter what one's religious inclination, as it addresses some of the most basic ideas of spirituality and morality that life presents us with.

Tao Te Ching

The Speed Read

The Tao is the river of life that exists before and after mankind. To restore harmony, practice inaction and find tranquillity. The Tao will resolve things naturally and the wise ruler who has refrained from incorrect action will be acclaimed by his people. The river takes the easiest path through the mountains and a valley is created. We come from nothingness and return to nothingness.

Letters on the Sufi Path, 1365–75
Ibn Abbad of Ronda

". . . the light of certitude. That is the most sublime thing that can descend from the heavens into the hearts of chosen believers, who comprehend thereby the Mystic Truth of the attributes and names."

T HE LITERATURE OF Islam is complex and wide-ranging, and it is far beyond the scope of this book to attempt any sort of systematic overview of that tradition. However, in Rumi's *Spiritual Couplets* and Ibn Abbad's *Letters on the Sufi Path* we see two contrasting examples of literature, each of which is interesting for the different light it casts on Islamic thought – Rumi takes a more extravagantly poetic approach whereas this book is a more thoughtful, precise meditation.

Both books are also from the tradition of Sufism. This is an area which has been popularized in the West, and which has probably been widely misunderstood in the process. The works of Idries Shah, which were especially popular a few decades ago, presented a rather new-age interpretation of Sufism in which it was depicted as an idea that was prior to and separate from Islam, and as a rather humanistic, mystical body of thought. As a result of such writings, Sufism has been a source of fascination in the West.

However it is also fair to observe that there are wide variations in opinion about Sufism within Islam. One of the tragedies of the modern age is that the West tends to perceive Islam as a unitary body of thought, and to see fundamentalists as representative of an entire, living religion that has as many subtle variations as Christianity itself does. The varying attitudes to Sufism are merely one example of a case where there is no single Islamic point of view. In some Islamic states the practices of Sufism have been banned or regarded as inappropriate, whereas other scholars have seen Sufism as an essential part of the tradition.

So what is Sufism? In short it is a body of thought and practice in which the inner, mystical path to God is emphasized more than external acts. There is a wide variety of ways in which this is expressed, ranging from the traditional whirling dervishes to more contemplative forms of spirituality. But in general, Sufism is defined by the believer who seeks to grow closer to God or even to become one with him, in the more esoteric or mystical strands of Sufism.

Ibn Abbad studied in the madrasahs of Morocco and became a member of the Shadhiliyah order of mystics in 1359. This was a time when the orthodox religious leaders of Morocco were somewhat divided. The Shadhiliyah order represented a relatively moderate form of mysticism within Islam, in which the inner life was emphasized but only within the context of ordinary everyday practice. Ibn Abbad was able to become an imam and lead public prayers in the country. As such he became well known as a spiritual leader.

The letters included in this collection were written from the small town of Sale to friends of Ibn Abbad's in the main city. They were designed to answer questions about the fundamentals of Sufi spirituality for believers who were troubled or uncertain about their religious ideas or had specific queries.

The subjects dealt with are eminently practical ones. For instance one is "a letter concerning the actions and spiritual states required of a penitent if he is to be confirmed in the station of repentance" while another addresses "the question of Pilgrimage and its legal requirements in relation to individuals and circum-stances." Thus they provide a fascinating insight into the practices of Islam and Sufism in this period, and into the root ideas that underpin this religious tradition.

This is not a poetic tour de force like the work of Rumi. Nor is it the mystical pantheism that one might expect from Sufism if one relied on Idries Shah as one's guide. Instead it is an example of Sufism as a simple everyday religious practice in which one approaches Godliness by focusing on practical matters and the spiritual wellbeing that one can achieve in everyday life.

Ibn Abbad has been compared to St John of the Cross. While there are many differences between the two figures, they do share an emphasis on the ways in which everyday virtue and practice can move us closer to God in our hearts. As such, this is an enlightening book for anyone to read, regardless of their religious background, and a useful insight into the Islamic tradition of which the West, in general, knows so little.

Letters on the Sufi Path

The Speed Read

Fifty four letters from Ibn Abbad of Ronda to his followers regarding their spiritual problems and practical religious thoughts. A tantalizing glimpse of the Sufism as a mystical part of the Islamic culture of the past and present.

Spiritual Couplets, Thirteenth Century
Rumi

*"When you do things from your soul, you feel a river
moving in you, a joy."*

RUMI WAS A thirteenth-century Persian Muslim poet and theologian. His full name, Jalal ad-Din Muhammad Rumi roughly translates as "Majesty of Religion." He was born in present-day Afghanistan and died in Turkey, but both areas were at the time part of Persia, in the Seljuk Empire, and he wrote in the Persian language. He is regarded as a classic spiritual writer within the overlapping traditions of Islam and Sufism, and is widely read today in Iran, Afghanistan, and other areas that retain a Persian influence. He is also remembered as the inspiration behind the Mevlevi Order, better known to the West as the Whirling Dervishes, who express their religious worship through a musical and dance ceremony known as the *sema*.

His major poetic and spiritual work is the *Masnavi* or *Masnavi-I Ma'navi.* The title means "Rhyming Couplets of Profound Spiritual Meaning" but it is often published under the title *Spiritual Couplets.* This is a vast work that includes elements of fable, everyday anecdotes, scriptural reference to the Qu'ran, and metaphysical speculation. It has been described as the Persian Qu'ran, but it is a more intensely poetical work than a piece of scripture. And while Rumi is writing within the Islamic tradition, his thoughts have a universal appeal. He saw religion as an intensely personal experience and focused on the role of the soul, the act of creative love, and our desire to be reunited with God.

He writes about the concept of Tawhid (unity), a common theme in Sufism, which centers on the idea that we have been cut off from union with the beloved, the divinity, and spend our lives trying to seek union. He saw creative acts such as music, dancing and poetry as deep expressions of the soul's love for God, and this was the inspiration behind his development of ideas that would influence the Whirling Dervishes.

Within the Mevlevi tradition, the ceremony of sema represents an attempt to seek truth and perfection by abandoning the ego and loving all creation. This idea of spiritual growth through creativity and transcendence of the self is something that goes beyond specific religions – Rumi is often quoted by thinkers as varied as Zen masters, Christian theologians, and modern Islamic scholars.

In the theology of Rumi, man is separated from the Divine ego, and is then compelled to follow an evolutionary journey back towards union with the Divine. The fall of Adam is interpreted within this context as man's initial separation from God. Through an evolutionary and creative process, we then seek to return to God, meaning that God is the goal of all existence. The universal, yet personal nature of Rumi's thought can be illustrated with a quote from his work:

> *I searched for God among the Christians and on the Cross and therein I found Him not.*
>
> *I went into the ancient temples of idolatry; no trace of Him was there.*
>
> *I entered the mountain cave of Hira and then went as far as Qandhar but God I found not.*
>
> *With set purpose I fared to the summit of Mount Caucasus and found there only 'anqa's habitation.*
>
> *Then I directed my search to the Kaaba, the resort of old and young; God was not there even.*
>
> *Turning to philosophy I inquired about him from Ibn Sina but found Him not within his range.*
>
> *I fared then to the scene of the Prophet's experience of a great divine*

*manifestation only a 'two bow-lengths' distance from him' but
God was not there even in that exalted court.
Finally, I looked into my own heart and there I saw Him; He was
nowhere else.*

Rumi is neither accepting nor rejecting the traditional religions in his writing, and his writing must be understood as part of the Islamic tradition. However his focus on the personal nature of the search for God gives his writing a universal appeal. In the final analysis, God is located in our hearts and only by exploring our hearts will we be reunited with him.

Another aspect of Rumi that shouldn't be ignored is the degree to which he represents the great Persian tradition of thought. The vexed relationship between Iran and other countries in the region and the West in the last century probably means that we have less understanding of Persian traditions than we do, for instance, of the religious texts of Japan, India, and China. Rumi is both an ideal starting place for a glimpse into Persian tradition, and a reminder that there is a beautiful, sometimes underestimated, poetic and spiritual tradition in the region.

Modern day Iranians are as familiar with Rumi's work as many Westerners are with Shakespeare or Milton. Rumi's popularity has grown in the West, but he is nonetheless a spiritual writer who could be better known and appreciated.

Spiritual Couplets

The Speed Read

The thirteenth-century poetic Persian classic. We are separated from God and spend our lives seeking to be reunited with him. We can be helped in this quest by religious scripture but in the end the search must begin in our own hearts. Through music, poetry, and dance, we can overcome the ego and start the search for God in our souls.

Siddhartha, 1922

Hermann Hesse

*"Wisdom is not communicable. The wisdom which a wise man
tries to communicate always sounds foolish. . . . Knowledge
can be communicated but not wisdom. One can find it, live it, be
fortified by it, do wonders through it, but one cannot
communicate and teach it."*

HERMANN HESSE is an author whose reputation has
waned somewhat over the last few decades. A popular
German writer from the pre-war period onwards, he
attained a rather trendy reputation with the 1960s generation,
partly as a result of the hallucinatory imagery of his novel
Steppenwolf, and partly because of his dabbling with Eastern
spirituality.

Since then he has been subjected to a critical re-evaluation and
many feel that his work was somewhat over-rated. However, there
is still much to admire in his writing. And *Siddhartha,* one of his
most explicitly spiritual books, is a novel that is worth reading at
different stages of life – it often reads rather differently to young
people than it does to those who have more life experience, but
both can find interesting messages in its narrative.

The book grew out of Hesse's fascination with Indian religion.
It deals with themes from both the Hindu and Buddhist traditions,
and while Hesse pursues his own ideas, sometimes at the cost of
accuracy to the source religions, he overall gives a reasonably
accurate impression of aspects of those traditions.

Siddhartha is the book's hero. In a plot that skips to and fro in time, we encounter him as an old ferryman, who spends his time observing and listening to the river. Once he was a wandering wise man, and a follower of Gotama the Buddha. (The Buddha was actually called Siddhartha Gautama, and many people have taken the book to be an allegory of his life, although Hesse's actual intentions are clearly to set Siddhartha up as a separate figure in his own right – the fact that Gotama appears as a character in the book makes this clear).

Siddhartha was the son of a Brahmin, a handsome, wise, charismatic man who became a religious adept at an early age. In spite of the all the worldly opportunities open to him, he left home in the company of his close friend Govinda to pursue a life of asceticism. They are in search of enlightenment.

The two friends encounter Gotama the Buddha, and spend time with him. Govinda vows to stay with him, but Siddhartha believes that his enlightenment must be something he achieves alone, so the two friends part.

Siddhartha goes on to plunge back into the world of earthly wealth and pleasures, after meeting the courtesan Kamala, with whom he fathers a son. She introduces him to a merchant who is her friend, and Siddhartha becomes a rich man. He takes his place among the "child people" who are not interested in enlightenment, only in worldly things.

Through this process Hesse discusses the concept of *samsara*. The river, which is a recurring metaphor in the book, refers to the Indian concept of the flow of life – samsara refers to the constant flow of the world into which we may be reincarnated, and in which we experience suffering and evil – it is a different version of the idea of the "circle of life." By plunging himself into the world of pleasure and money, Siddhartha is pursuing a different approach to knowledge, but one that means nothing to him until he realizes the worthlessness of this life.

It is once he starts to suffer from the sickness of the soul, which Hesse describes as being the characteristic feature of the wealthy, that Siddhartha leaves all that he has attained behind. He meets with the ferryman who helps him across the river for free, and eventually Siddhartha will himself come to tend the riverboat.

Late in the book, Siddhartha encounters the son that he didn't know he had, after the death of Kamala who was on a pilgrimage to meet the Buddha. Here we encounter a different version of the circle of life, as Siddhartha's son turns out to be ungrateful and difficult, while Siddhartha himself finds that he doesn't know how to deal with this young man. Just as the young Siddhartha was self-willed enough to leave home in search of enlightenment, he discovers that his own son is also unwilling to learn from his elders.

It is by putting all the different aspects of his experience in the world together that Siddhartha finally finds a form of wisdom. He finds himself in rhythm with the spirit of the passing river. This is the discovery with which Siddhartha reaches his own epiphany and becomes adjusted to the spiritual problems and achievements of his own life.

There are different ways of viewing this book. Young readers tend to react to Siddhartha's stubborn sense of individualism and his desire to work things out for himself. The fact that his progress to enlightenment is such a difficult one is perhaps not the first moral that one draws from the book.

To older readers, the idealism of the early parts of Siddhartha's life, and some of Hesse's religious ideas can seem naïve and simplistic. However there is still much to appreciate in his description of a life of spiritual development. Even his rather brattish child comes with an interesting moral – he is an unappealing character, but one that brings out the fact that even someone who has learned a great deal can struggle when faced with new challenges, especially within the family.

As an explication of Hindu and Buddhist thought the book has many obvious faults. Hesse gives some fair explanations of ideas such as samsara and nirvana, but his concept of these religions is far more individualistic than most experts would allow. Siddhartha's journey is not a Buddhist one to escape from the self. It is more of an attempt to discover the self – and his final epiphany is not one that escapes from this self-centered approach.

But the fact that one can pick fault does not mean that this isn't a rewarding read. It is a book that provokes one to argue with Hesse, to think about the concepts that he is discussing and, perhaps, to go and discover more about Eastern religion, from less maverick sources. In the end it is a novel and as such should not be treated to the same analysis as a theological textbook. But it is an interesting book and one that can provoke serious thought at any stage of life.

Siddhartha

The Speed Read

Siddhartha sat by the river, contemplating the flow of life. As a child he had run away from a life of privilege to seek enlightenment. After his friend Govinda stayed with Gotama the Buddha, someone that Siddhartha admired but would not join as a follower, Siddhartha plunged in a decadent world of wealth and pleasure. When his soul sickened as a result, he left it all behind and ended up back here by the river. Then his son came to visit him, and it all went badly wrong, but it all helps to show how that old river keeps on flowing by.

The Prophet, 1923
Kahlil Gibran

"Life is indeed darkness save when there is urge,
And all urge is blind save when there is knowledge,
And all knowledge is vain save when there is work,
And all work is empty save when there is love."

*T*HE PROPHET IS THE best known book of Kahlil Gibran, who was born Lebanese, but whose family emigrated to the United States in 1895. Gibran became well known as an artist, studying in Boston and New York, but over time it was his writing that made him more famous.

Written in 1923, *The Prophet* is a collection of poetic essays which center on a fictional prophet called Almustufa. The prophet has been away from his home in the city Orphalese for a long time, but now chooses to return home. On his journey he discusses his ideas with a group of people that he meets. Religion and spirituality were natural subjects for Gibran. He was fascinated by a variety of theological subjects, such as the schism that had occurred between the Orthodox and Catholic traditions, and in the similarities that can be found in all religions in spite of the enmities that often exist between those religions.

The prophet teaches the people he meets about his ideas on a range of subjects, including world religion and the state of being a human. He also talks about more everyday subjects such as love, work, learning and marriage. His thoughts are simple but often quite inspiring. And throughout the language used by Gibran to express the prophet's thoughts is beautiful and poetic.

A strong theme of Gibran's thought is an ecumenical attempt to find common ground amongst religions and to interpret the thinking of Jesus in the light of this. He concurs with Jesus's reaction to the harsher forms of Old Testament scripture, arguing that "an eye for an eye, and the whole world would be blind." He also follows Jesus in emphasizing the importance of love, writing passages such as this:

> *Love gives naught but itself and takes naught but from itself.*
> *Love possesses not nor would it be possessed;*
> *For love is sufficient unto love.*

In trying to find common ecumenical ground, the ideas in the book are occasionally slightly vague. He writes, "I love you when you bow in your mosque, kneel in your temple, pray in your church. For you and I are sons of one religion, and it is the spirit." At times one feels that Gibran is over-reaching, attempting to create a new scripture that could unite different traditions, without truly comprehending the elements that make those traditions separate. One is reminded of the thinking of C.S. Lewis, who respected different religious traditions but rejected ecumenical ideas on the basis that different religions do indeed bring different aspects of thought to the world they inhabit.

Gibran was personally intrigued by the Bahá'í faith and its emphasis on the spiritual unity of mankind. It has been reported that Abdul-Bahá was one of the models that he was thinking of in his creation of the prophet. This was one reason for the book's emphasis on the unity and similarity of different kinds of faith around the world.

Another aspect of *The Prophet* is Gibran's emphasis on a more sensual understanding of the world. At one point he writes that we should "forget not that the earth delights to feel your bare feet and the winds long to play with your hair." Here, one can't help but be reminded of a very different religious thinker,

William Blake, who argued that the organized church had turned against the energy and will of the body and decreed that all sensual enjoyment was evil. Gibran would side with Blake at least in so far as he believed that sensual feelings could be a positive force.

It is hard to summarize *The Prophet* briefly. Perhaps this is a result of the worst fault of the book, a tendency to woolly vagueness rather than precise statements. The poetry of the book can conceal some indeterminate ideas. On the other hand Gibran himself argues that perplexity is the first step towards knowledge. He suggests that our confusion about the world is itself a positive thing as it forces us to try to understand the world in all its complexity.

Gibran is also a powerful advocate for the idea that love and beauty can be important aims of human endeavour as well as simple truth. In pursuit of this ideal, one has to admit that in *The Prophet* the author succeeds in creating a work of beauty. It may not have the profundity that it can appear to have on the surface, and re-readings of the book might lead one to conclude that it is shallow in some respects, while appearing to be deep. But it can be a consoling and charming book to read and will be one from which different people will take different messages.

The Prophet

The Speed Read

On the way back to his home, the prophet Almustafa stopped to share his great wisdom. He told us to believe in truth and beauty, and that all of mankind seeks God, even if we do so through different faiths and methods. Above all he told us many beautiful things about love, some of which are a bit hard to remember in retrospect, but they seemed lovely at the time.

Essays in Zen Buddhism, 1927–34
D.T. Suzuki

"The truth of Zen, just a little bit of it, is what turns one's hum drum life, a life of monotonous, uninspiring commonplaceness, into one of art, full of genuine inner creativity."

THERE IS A PROBLEM with Zen Buddhism. The degree to which it took off as a trendy form of Eastern religion in the West during the twentieth century means that it has acquired a slightly strange reputation and has been misrepresented by sources as varied as Robert M. Pirsig's *Zen and The Art of Motorcycle Maintenance* and Jack Kerouac's *Satori in Paris.*

As a result it is hard to write about Zen from basics – there is so much baggage attached to its Western interpretation that it can be hard to set this to one side and attempt to understand the real tradition. One remedy for this might be to return to work of D.T. Suzuki. Suzuki was the first great champion of Zen in the West, and while his own work can be accused of containing certain distortions, returning to it at least allows us to trace the history of the idea in Western culture.

Zen is a branch of Mahayana Buddhism which grew (as *Chan*) in China in the seventh century and spread throughout the region, reaching Japan where it was called Zen. While it is a part of traditional Buddhist tradition and shares much with other branches of the religion, it places more emphasis on dharma practice and the wisdom of experience than it does on scriptural sources and teachers. The form of meditation know as *zazen* is directed towards awakening, through meditation and contemplation.

Suzuki (1870–1966) grew up in a Japanese family that practiced Jodo Shinshu Buddhism, but went on to study a wide variety of strands of Buddhism in his youth. He studied under the Zen master Shaku Soen, who was unusual among his contemporaries for having traveled to Indian and Ceylon to experience Theravada and Pali Buddhist schools. Suzuki spent four years studying under Shaku Soen, though he was not a fully ordained Zen monk.

In the 1890s, Shaku Soen traveled to the United States to participate in a religious conference. When he was asked to help a local academic with translations of Eastern religious texts, he recommended Suzuki for the task, and this was the start of a long and illustrious career for Suzuki in which he translated many Eastern titles for the Western market, and also wrote erudite explanations of Eastern ways of thought.

Suzuki wrote the *Essays on Zen Buddhism* in the 1920s and 1930s. Some of his shorter works address the same material but there is a rich diversity of material in these volumes that conveys the full range of his thinking. It is interesting to note that Suzuki retained a great fascination for Jodo Shinshu Buddhism, but for the most part focused intentionally on Zen in his Western writings.

Part of the reason for this was apparently the fact that he thought Zen better suited to the Western mind. The fact that Zen is less reliant on knowledge of past masters and scriptures certainly makes it something appealing to the impatient Western mind, and the many amusing tales of Zen masters and their relations with pupils also make it a memorable religion to study. But it seems highly relevant that, for Suzuki, Zen was not the greatest or only expression of Buddhist thought, just the one he chose to focus on in terms of Western readers.

It is also interesting to note a difference of opinion between Suzuki and his Zen master Shaku Soen, whose writings emphasized that Zen was essentially a branch of Mahayana Buddhism. By contrast Suzuki believed that Zen had absorbed a great deal from Taoism in China. He also liked to draw parallels with western thinkers such as Meister Eckhart.

This part of his thinking was extremely influential in the 1950s and 1960s as Zen became popular in the West – Zen was often interpreted as though it was a solitary outpost of Buddhism, with more in common with other mystical religious practices rather than as part of a living religion.

Suzuki also focused on the idea of *satori* (awakening) as the goal of Zen training, and he wrote a great deal about the way that in Japanese and Chinese culture this had developed within the everyday routines of monastic routine – so that satori might arise from mundane tasks such as gardening or carpentry, or even housekeeping. This element of his thought was a clear influence on those Western thinkers who tried to reinterpret Zen in a wide variety of everyday practices from archery to motorcycle maintenance.

D.T.Suzuki was a wise man and someone who brought a wide variety of Eastern sources to Western attention through his writings and translations. He is also a brilliant writer, and one can take a great deal from his essays on Zen and other books. Anyone interested in Buddhism or Zen would be well advised to start from his writings, as they are an excellent source.

However, there is a second reason to start any study of Zen in the Western tradition from his writing. This is the fact that he has been so utterly influential on the Western tradition. One needs to understand that much of the Western idea of Zen is in fact an interpretation of one man's views on the subject, and that he came at the subject from a specific angle, one that emphasized certain aspects of the "eastern mind," and that brought a uniquely Japanese viewpoint to the study of a religion that originated in China.

Zen, and Suzuki's writing on Zen, has influenced many Westerners over the last few decades. Many people will find his work, and that of others who have interpreted Zen, deeply inspiring and spiritual. This in itself makes him someone that has played a valuable role. For those who wish to truly understand Zen, it may be worth bearing in mind that this is a tradition that goes far beyond the Western version of it, and that a wider variety of sources will need to be studied to achieve a deeper under-standing of its real meaning.

Essays in Zen Buddhism

The Speed Read

A scholarly, brilliant exposition of Zen Buddhism as D.T. Suzuki understood it. A superb resource for anyone interested in Zen, and in some senses an antidote to the bowdlerizations that have followed in his wake in popular culture. But also this is only one source among many and even this wise master can't tell us everything we might need to know to understand Zen.

The Teachings of Don Juan:
A Yaqui Way of Knowledge, 1968
Carlos Castaneda

"Look at every path closely and deliberately, then ask ourselves this crucial question: Does this path have a heart? If it does, then the path is good. If it doesn't, it is of no use."

IT SEEMS ALMOST too obvious a fact to state, but not all books about spirituality are to be trusted, even when they have acquired the status of "classics" to some readers. The mystical works of Carlos Castaneda have sold millions of copies and were extremely popular in the later 1960s and 1970s. However later researchers have created serious doubt as to whether his work was fact or fiction, and it is best to be aware of those claims when considering his writing.

His first book, *The Teachings of Don Juan*, was published in 1968, and a series of sequels was to follow over subsequent years. The books describe Castaneda's research and knowledge of shamanic practices, which he claimed to have acquired from a traditional wise man, Don Juan Matus, a Yaqui Indian from the north of Mexico. Don Juan was supposed to have identified Castaneda as having the energy of a "nagual," and thus able to be chosen by the spirit to become a leader of seers. He wrote often of the way that shamanic practice could allow one to expand one's perception to realms that are usually unknown to humans. He spoke of this "nonordinary" realm as something that was real but only obtainable to those who could learn new ways of perceiving.

Strange experiences abound in the books, from Castaneda's

transformations into animals such as crows and his travels to alternate dimensions and meetings with spirits and witches. The books vary as to the importance of using psychotropic drugs to achieve an understanding of this nonordinary realm, but Castaneda describes the use of peyote and other natural drugs to achieve altered states of consciousness.

Castaneda's work includes a good deal of authentic detail about shamanic practices. He was awarded academic qualifications on the basis of his research, and many anthropologists accepted his work as sincere in the years after publication. However in 1976 Richard de Mille and Daniel Noel published sceptical investigations, and from then onward a stream of scholars who analyzed the books started to point out inconsistencies and problems.

The books seem to contain discrepancies in terms of time and narrative, and there are alternative published sources for everything that Castaneda wrote (critics particularly point to the degree to which his writing appears to draw on Barbara Myerhoff's work). Also, no one was able to locate any likely suspect for the figure of Don Juan himself.

The most damning evidence of all was probably the work de Mille did on Castaneda's library requests which show that at times when he claimed to have been present at peyote ceremonies, he was actually in the library of the University of California reading books that described such ceremonies.

Castaneda's life went on to become more complicated with the Tensegrity movement he later founded to promote shamanic practices, and his rather odd personal life, living with a gaggle of "witches" who proved very difficult to trace after his death.

None of this has prevented his books from continuing to sell. Some modern readers enjoy them on the basis that they are fiction, but enjoyable and fascinating to read. Others accept that his accounts are questionable but see the books as powerful works of philosophy and spirituality in spite of that, while others now regard Castaneda as a mere charlatan who piggybacked on the work of others to create a fraudulent body of work.

Can one find enlightenment in work that appears to have a

dubious provenance? Certainly some people might think so, and Castaneda's work has clearly inspired devotion and fascination in many readers over the years. It now seems characteristic of the period in which the works were first published that Castaneda convinced many to trust him on the basis of his charisma and evident powers of persuasion. The 1960s and 1970s are remembered as times of new ideas and experimentation and it was inevitable that some of the thinkers and communicators of the time would be opportunistic in taking advantage of the credulity that was engendered.

If one reads Castaneda today it is perhaps best to view the books as charming, intriguing journeys into one man's dreams and imagination rather than as genuine accounts of shamanism. On this basis they can be entertaining reads, but rather than guides to authentic spirituality they become relics of strange period of history, when people wanted to believe in something new and exciting, no matter how ludicrous it might be.

The Teachings of Don Juan

The Speed Read

I traveled to Mexico and met Don Juan, a Yaqui Indian man of knowledge. He taught me many amazing things, such as becoming a crow, seeing spirits, taking copious amounts of peyote, and other feats of spiritual wonder. Trust me, this is all true . . .

Be Here Now, 1971
Ram Dass

"It is important to expect nothing, to take every experience, including the negative ones, as merely steps on the path, and to proceed."

R AM DASS IS NOW known as a guru, a teacher of spiritual ideas, in particular those of Eastern religion. However he started out as a successful psychologist in the Western tradition. He was called Richard Alpert, born 1931, and was teaching at Harvard in the early 1960s when he became fascinated by hallucinogenic drugs and their effects on the mind.

Of his own use of the drugs, he later wrote: "Psychedelics helped me to escape . . . albeit momentarily . . . from the prison of my mind. It over-rode the habit patterns of thought and I was able to taste innocence again. Looking at sensations freshly without the conceptual overlay was very profound."

This was in the early days of LSD when it was quite common for intellectuals to become interested in the ways in which the drug altered consciousness and at least appeared to offer insights into the way that the mind worked. Alpert was in fairly esteemed company – he worked with Allen Ginsberg, Aldous Huxley, and Timothy Leary, amongst others. It was Leary that introduced Alpert to teonanácatl, the Mexican psychoactive mushroom, after Alpert flew them to Mexico in his private plane.

However, the Harvard establishment was less open to the idea of drug-induced enlightenment, and Alpert was dismissed from his post as a result of his work. He went on to study yoga, meditation, and other spiritual practices. He became an environmental and

political campaigner and also a devotee of the Indian guru Neem
Karoli Baba, a Hindu adept of bhakti yoga and regarded service
to others (*seva*) as the ultimate form of unconditional love for to
God.

After Alpert changed his name to Ram Dass, he would help
found the Seva Foundation which aimed to abolish world poverty.
Neem Karoli also practiced a very inclusive form of teaching – in
spite of India's caste system and natural tendency to hierarchical
social practices, he preferred to make his students feel like part of
the process, and to believe that their contributions were as valid as
anyone else's. This is an attitude that Dass took into his own
teaching.

In some respects one can see Ram Dass as a fairly typical
exponent of the mystical, optimistic ideas that were in fashion in
the 1960s. But that would be to underestimate the subtlety of his
thinking. His writing has developed over the years and he has the
wisdom to be able to acknowledge where his early work was
influenced more by the zeitgeist than by genuine revelation. One
of his late books *One-Liners*, brings his story up to date and shows a
funny, likeable man who can understand his own failings, but who
still has a real message of love.

However it was *Be Here Now*, published in 1971, that initially
made Dass' reputation. The book has sold over a million copies,
but was originally distributed as a pamphlet by the Lama
Foundation, a commune in New Mexico whose founders were
friends with Dass. The Lama Foundation later gave the copyright
and an equal share of the proceeds to the Hanuman Foundation,
another of Dass' ventures that worked to further his spiritual
aims.

The book is divided into four parts. The first part tells the story
of Richard Alpert's journey to becoming Baba Ram Dass. He is
open about his use of psychedelic drugs but the general drive of
the book is to look for alternative ways, through yoga and other
spiritual practices, to find the kinds of revelations that Dass had
first experienced through drugs. In the second part of the book,
Dass includes a series of rather lovely aphorisms on the spiritual

life, together with his own illustrations. In the third part, Dass examines various practices, including yoga and meditation, through which one can make spiritual progress. Finally, in the last section, Dass recommends writings and texts that might help one to discover one's own spiritual path.

As ever, Dass is not remotely prescriptive in his teaching. He puts his own life forward as an example, but allows us to see his faults as well as his achievements. And he understands that his path may not work for everyone. This is one of the aspects of his writing that gives it a particular charm, and is arguably the most important thing he learned from his own guru Neem Karoli Baba. One of the sections of the book deals very directly with the ways in which the student–teacher relationship can both help and hinder both sides of the equation.

Be Here Now continues to sell to this day. Ram Dass has continued to write over the years, but this is the book that most clearly encapsulates his early espousal of Eastern religious techniques as a path to a more enlightened life. It was also a book that had some positive influence at the time, as the chimerical idea that drugs would lead to enlightenment became more and more obviously a dangerous idea that had led many into damaging themselves through addiction or psychosis.

By putting himself forward as someone who had learned from drugs but who had moved on to a yogic lifestyle, Dass was sending an important message to the post-hippy community. He showed that it was possible to come from a drug-influenced background, to learn from that background and then move on to safer, more positive ways of "freeing one's mind." Now that most people recognize the dangers of drugs more clearly, *Be Here Now* works both as a testament to the mood of its times, and as a lesson in alternative routes to enlightenment.

Ram Dass' legacy is not restricted to his writings. He also has a powerful record of continuing to try and effect positive change in the world through the various foundations with which he is associated. If one can judge a man on the life he has lived, then Ram Dass is someone who deserves great respect.

Be Here Now

The Speed Read

I am just a beginner on the path to enlightenment, but I am here to share the little I have learned with you. I took a lot of acid and drew these crazy pictures, but now I continue my journey through yoga and meditation, as I learned to do from my Hindu guru. Each of us finds their own way, and their own way of sharing what little wisdom we might acquire. "Our rational minds can never understand what has happened, but our hearts . . . if we can keep them open to God, will find their own intuitive way."

The Power of Now, 1999
Eckhart Tolle

"Being is the eternal, ever-present One Life beyond the myriad forms of life that are subject to birth and death. However, Being is not only beyond but also deep within every form as its innermost invisible and indestructible essence. This means that it is accessible to you now as your own deepest self, your true nature."

A GREAT MANY self-help and new-age books have some degree of spiritual content. We have not included many of these in this collection because all too often the spiritual content seems rather shallow. *The Power of Now* is an interesting book because in many ways it seems to be a kind of self-help manual, and Tolle's books are lauded by Oprah Winfrey, but in fact his writing does address some real spiritual concerns in an interesting way.

Tolle was born in Germany and lived in Spain and England as a young man, before moving to Canada. He had a rather solitary childhood and suffered from depression in his twenties before undergoing what he refers to as an "inner transformation" at the age of 29.

The Power of Now begins with an account of this moment and the way in which it moved him out of a period of suicidal anxiety. The book teaches that we are too absorbed in "doing" rather than "being" and that we become too absorbed by the past and the future, to the degree that we lose sight of the importance of the Now.

He talks about the ego, using the psychological idea in a slightly different way to classical Freudian analysis. For Tolle, the ego is the construction we have of what we believe our self to be. So the past is the story on which we base our idea of self, while the future rules us because we are always driven by our ego to seek future resolution of problems. He sees all problems as illusions caused by our way of perception of time and ego.

So we reject the present to dwell on the past, whether it is a sad or happy past because that is the story we allow to define us. And we reject the present to dwell on the future, something which merely adds to our anxieties because no matter what schemes and ambitions we have for the future, we know it will end in our deaths.

So Tolle argues that the way to escape these traps is to live more fully in the Now. Rather than believing in the ego we have constructed, we need to react directly to the world as we see it now, and to transcend the ego. The emotional "pain body" we have built is also a function of time and our inability to free ourselves from attachments.

Of course this is related to Buddhist concepts of detachment from existence. Tolle doesn't advocate any specific religious path as his focus is on the individual's place in the world, but anyone familiar with Buddhist literature will see some parallels. But for Tolle, the goal isn't extinction of the self in nirvana. Instead he argues that we have an underlying identity, an "I Am" which is simply the part of us that perceives the now in stillness and without interpreting it through the ego.

Analysts might argue that the id, which he seems to be referring to, is not a reliable thing to regress to in our search for spiritual peace. Buddhists might object that he retains too much sense of self. But his argument is quite persuasive, and relies on other influences. He has acknowledged influences such as Krishnamurti, Meister Eckhart, and the *Tao Te Ching* on his writing. He also respects the teaching of the New Testament but believes that Jesus' teaching is often misunderstood. He sees love as something that can only arise from a true recognition of one's underlying self rather than from reliance on the ego.

In Tolle's other books, such as *Stillness Speaks* and *A New Earth,* he develops his ideas further, but *The Power of Now* remains the best introduction to his work as it expresses his most basic ideas in a powerful way. The book will appeal most to those who are suffering from depression or other crises as it promises a way to solve such problems. For this reason it can be compared to self-help manuals in general.

However the way that Tolle speaks of the construction of the ego is quite interesting for anyone interested in spirituality. In the end, many religious and spiritual teachers show us that either introspection or a retreat from the world can bring us a deeper understanding of ourselves and our relationship with the world. Such ideas can encourage unhealthy levels of self-absorption, but so long as one is aware of this danger, they can also lead us to a genuine breakthrough in understanding the things that make up our idea of ourselves.

In *Walden,* Thoreau suggests setting aside material things in order to find a simpler way of life, and the eremitic tradition suggests that solitude is the path that will lead us to God. Tolle's teaching is related to such ideas, but he is offering us a framework within which we can examine the way we think about the world, and the degree to which our thoughts of past and future define our ego. Understanding this can genuinely help us to focus more on the present moment and perhaps to react more authentically to the world around us.

The Power of Now

The Speed Read

People allow themselves to be distracted by thinking about time – the past creates a story upon which we base our ego creation. The future calls to us as we create desires and ambitions for our ego. All of this creates pain and emotion in the present and prevents us from appreciating and understanding the present as it happens. We need to transcend the ego to find our real selves and to engage with the world in a purer, simpler way.

Index by Author